Patrick Carnes, Ph.D.

A Gentle Path Through The Twelve Steps

a Guidebook

for All People

in the Process

of Recovery

CompCare® Publishers

2415 Annapolis Lane
Minneapolis, Minnesota 55441

ISBN 0-89638-161-7

Interior design by Pamela Arnold
Cover design by Lillian Svec
Electronic typesetting and production by Mark Stefan

Inquiries, orders, and catalog requests should be addressed to
CompCare Publishers
2415 Annapolis Lane
Minneapolis, Minnesota 55441
Call toll free 800/328-3330
(Minnesota residents 612/559-4800)

		3	4	5
90	91	92	93	

A note to those starting out on this gentle path: This guidebook has been designed with generous margins for note taking at the top of each page. Often in working a particular step, you or your program guides will have insights on another step or another aspect of your addiction and recovery. These margins will serve as a convenient place to record flashes of insight, feelings, and reminders.

It is hoped that this workbook can evolve and improve, as recovery can with effort. If you have any suggestions for improving the workbook, please send them to the author in care of CompCare Publishers. New editions can reflect the growth of all of us.

The Twelve Steps of Alcoholics Anonymous

STEP ONE
We admitted we were powerless over alcohol—that our lives had become unmanageable.

STEP TWO
Came to believe that a Power greater than ourselves could restore us to sanity.

STEP THREE
Made a decision to turn our will and our lives over to the care of God *as we understood Him.*

STEP FOUR
Made a searching and fearless moral inventory of ourselves.

STEP FIVE
Admitted to God, to ourselves, and to another human being the exact nature of our wrongs.

STEP SIX
Were entirely ready to have God remove all these defects of character.

STEP SEVEN
Humbly asked Him to remove our shortcomings.

STEP EIGHT
Made a list of all persons we had harmed, and became willing to make amends to all of them.

STEP NINE
Made direct amends to such people wherever possible,
except when to do so would injure them or others.

STEP TEN
Continued to take personal inventory, and when we were wrong, promptly admitted it.

STEP ELEVEN
Sought through prayer and meditation to improve our conscious contact with God
as we understood Him, praying only for knowledge of His will for us
and the power to carry that through.

STEP TWELVE
Having had a spiritual awakening as the result of these steps,
we tried to carry this message to alcoholics and to practice
these principles in all our affairs.

The Twelve Steps reprinted with permission of Alcoholics Anonymous World Services, Inc. The program described in this work is not associated in any way with Alcoholics Anonymous.

Contents

Introduction

This workbook and the accompanying tape set* were designed to help people with different types of addictions, including alcoholics, gamblers, compulsive overeaters, and sex addicts, as well as their co-addicted loved ones. Many books exist to help recovering people through the Twelve Steps; some of them even address multiple addictions. This workbook, however, provides a unique set of structured forms and exercises to help you as a recovering person integrate the Twelve Steps into your life.

Gentleness becomes the theme for both the workbook and the audiotape workshop. Addiction by definition possesses a driven quality. Some recovering people try to work the Twelve Steps in the same compulsive manner with which they approached their lives. The spirit of the Twelve Steps is gentleness. The path is a gentle way. Like water wearing down hard rock, consistency and time become allies in creating new channels for one's life.

I hope that the workbook becomes for you a living document which records the basic elements of your story and your recovery. A workbook well used will be filled out completely, frayed at the edges, and have margins crowded with notes. Then, like the Velveteen Rabbit that came alive with use, your "living document" can bring vitality to your program. It can be a way for you to think through issues as you share them with your Twelve Step group, sponsor, therapist, therapy group, or significant others.

Anonymity or confidentiality prevents me from identifying the many people whose suggestions have improved this book of "forms." I am deeply grateful to all of you.

—P.J.C.

*Note from the publisher: You may have purchased this book separately from the cassettes. If you wish to obtain the accompanying audiotapes, please see the last page of this book for information on how to order.

Some Words about Working the Program

Although new members of Twelve Step programs often hear about "working the program," just what that means is often unclear. Each fellowship has its own definition. A bulimic, worried about bingeing, gets one response; an alcoholic, who wants a drink, gets a different one. Even in the same kind of fellowship (say AA or OA) groups vary according to members' ages, experience, and backgrounds. But some common elements exist that seem to transcend the various fellowships.

Going to Twelve Step meetings is the basic building block of recovery. Any meeting will help. Usually, a recovering person tries to attend one or two meetings a week, every week. Becoming involved with the life of those meetings provides a solid foundation for recovery. Making step presentations in the meetings or taking on group responsibilities, such as treasurer or group representative, are good ways for new members to become involved in the process. The time will come when any meeting will restore the serenity that goes with belonging to the fellowship, but for beginners, as well as experienced members, having a primary group or two anchors them in a program.

Much of working a program, however, goes on outside a meeting. Most recovering people learn about the program from applying program principles to their real life problems. Members of the group become consultants and teachers as a new member talks about the challenges of early recovery. Those relationships often last a long time. And even if they change, a recovering person learns how to get help from several sources and not face things alone. Twelve Step fellowships assist people with dependency problems in getting support and effective problem-solving.

Most groups also have a social life outside the meetings. Before or after meetings, people meet for coffee or food. Sometimes favorite restaurants become gathering spots. Some groups have regular breakfasts or lunches where people gather as sort of a "second" group meeting for extra support. Some groups have retreats together to intensify working on the program. While these are not part of the meeting, they are essential to program life. To regard them as an option one does not have time for is to miss out on an important part of developing a program for oneself: building a support network.

One major obstacle you as a new member may need to overcome is a reluctance to use the telephone. To feel comfortable only when talking about serious issues face to face limits your ability to use your consultants. Addicted people are not good at asking for help in general, and they will resist using a phone even at the most critical times. Thus they stay in their isolation. Using the phone can become a habit. At first it serves as a crisis hotline. As recovery progresses, it becomes a tool for maintaining and deepening intimacy. Some program veterans hold on to their phone phobias and still put together successful recoveries. They are rare, however. Many groups urge newcomers to get a phone list and make "practice" calls from the start.

A key figure in developing a program is your sponsor. The Twelve Steps in many ways are a demanding discipline. At whatever stage of recovery, early as well as advanced, new challenges emerge constantly in applying the steps. Recovering people select one (or sometimes two) sponsor who serves as a principal guide and witness. In early recovery, contact with a sponsor is often daily—and at times hourly. The sponsor does not have to be much more "expert" than you. Your sponsor is simply someone who:

— Agrees to be your sponsor;

— Knows your whole story;

— Can hold you accountable for how you work on your program;

— Keeps the focus on how the steps apply to your life;

— Can be honest with you;

— Will support you.

Sometimes sponsorship evolves into friendship, but the sponsor's chief goal is to help you understand your story. Sponsors also enhance their recoveries by helping you.

Twelve Step fellowships exist to help people stop self-destructive behavior over which they are powerless. Central to stopping the behavior is defining "sobriety." Sometimes that is difficult. What is a slip for a co-dependent or a compulsive eater? Does sobriety mean just abstinence for the alcoholic or is other behavior to be avoided as well? Most recovering people find that their understanding of "sobriety" evolves over time—and that it goes beyond just stopping self-destructive behavior. It also means embracing new behaviors. Later in this workbook you will have a chance to examine your definition of sobriety. At the outset, however, you will need to talk with your sponsor and your group about what you will not do. You may be powerless over your addiction, but you are responsible for your recovery.

Many people find initiating a recovery program extremely difficult. In earlier times the only solution when things got rough was to attend more meetings. Fortunately, professional therapists and treatment facilities now

---

support that process for the many forms of addictive illness. They have become extended partners to the fellowship. When you feel discouraged, read the "Big Book" of Alcoholics Anonymous—the original fellowship—especially chapters five and six. Composed in the days when professional support was unavailable and even hostile to Twelve Step groups, it serves as inspiration to all who wish to transform their lives.

The Twelve Steps form a process which promotes two qualities in its membership: honesty and spirituality. Starting with the first admission of powerlessness, the steps demand a high level of accountability to oneself and others. Only one way exists to maintain that level of integrity: a committed spirituality. The fellowship becomes a community that supports this process. The program, however, is not abstract but very concrete. You "work" your program whenever you:

— Make a call for support;

— Do a daily meditation on the program;

— Admit your powerlessness;

— Are honest about your mistakes and shortcomings;

— Have a spiritual awareness;

— Support another program person;

— Actively work on a step;

— Work for balance in your life;

— Focus on today;

— Take responsibility for your choices, feelings, and actions;

— Do something to mend harm you caused;

— Attend a meeting;

— Give a meeting;

— Maintain a defined sobriety.

Addicts and co-addicts live in the extremes. No middle ground exists. You, as an addict, are like a light switch which is either totally on or totally off. Life, however, requires a rheostat, that is, a switch mechanism in which there are various degrees of middle ground depending on the situation. Mental health involves a disciplined balance that relies on self-limits and boundaries. Nowhere is that more evident than in the two core issues that all addicts (including co-addicts) face: intimacy and dependency.

The most obvious extreme is dependency on a mood-altering drug or experience (like sex, gambling, or eating) to cope with life. The chemical or the experience becomes the only source of nurturing that is trusted and the primary focus of life for which everything else is sacrificed or compromised. This out-of-control experience or "powerlessness" makes life unmanageable and chaotic.

For every out-of-control experience, there is an opposite obsessive extreme grounded in overcontrol. With sexual obsession there are sexual addicts and there are those who are compulsively nonsexual. Many teetotallers are as obsessed in a negative way with alcohol as alcoholics are. A pattern clearly emerges of living in the extremes.

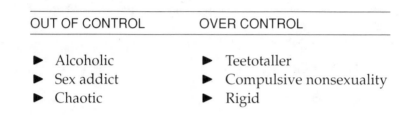

OUT OF CONTROL	OVER CONTROL
▶ Alcoholic	▶ Teetotaller
▶ Sex addict	▶ Compulsive nonsexuality
▶ Chaotic	▶ Rigid

When some of these obsessive behaviors mix, life becomes even more complex. Consider this couple: he is a sex addict and an alcoholic and she is a compulsive overeater. She attempts to control his addiction by throwing out his *Playboys* and his booze. He monitors her eating and criticizes her weight. They are both co-dependent. Each is obsessed with what the other is doing, each believing that he or she has the power to change the other. As his sex addiction becomes more out of control (although he believes he can control it), she becomes more nonsexual, acting as if she had the power to balance the equation. Even her excessive weight becomes a way to exert power by making herself sexually unattractive. The reality is they are both powerless in some ways they have not acknowledged.

Variations on this theme plague couples and families in which addiction thrives. A person can even live in simultaneous internal extremes. For example, think of the bulimic who both binges (overeats) and purges (vomits). Only one way exists for people to fight living in such addictive extremes: to admit to the reality of their powerlessness.

To accomplish that task, another issue needs to be faced: intimacy. Addicts and co-addicts seek closeness, nurturing, and love. In many ways addiction derives its compelling force because of a failure of intimacy. Addictive (again including co-addictive) obsession replaces human bonding and caring.

With no emotional rheostat, you can live an isolated, lonely existence in which you build walls around yourself, deny your own needs, and share nothing of yourself. Or, you flip to an emotionally enmeshed existence in which you are so overinvolved you feel trapped and smothered. You concentrate on meeting the needs of another person and take responsibility for that person's behavior. No boundaries exist and consequently no privacy exists. Again, a pattern of living in the extremes emerges.

ISOLATED	ENMESHED
► Denial of needs	► Needs of others are priority
► Lonely	► Smothered
► No sharing	► No privacy
► Alienated from others	► Responsible for others
► Extreme boundaries	► No boundaries

Add out of control with isolated—that's one extreme and you get off-center; add over control with enmeshed and you get off-center in another way.

ADDICTION/CO-ADDICTION

Extreme Living:

Out of Control	Over Control
Isolated	Enmeshed

RECOVERY

Centered Living:

Balance, Focus, Responsibility for Self

The Twelve Steps offer you a path out of extreme living. Three themes remain constant throughout the Twelve Step process: balance, focus, and responsibility for self.

Balance: to avoid either/or extremes.

Focus: to live in the present—a day at a time—not in the future, nor the past.

Responsibility for self: to live within your own human limits.

With these three themes as a basis for living your life, recovery becomes possible.

MY RECOVERY THEMES:

Balance

Focus

Responsibility for self

Before thoroughly pursuing your path, you need to secure guides to support you and help you find your way. Usually this starts with your sponsor. A sponsor is a person who works with you to help you understand the program you undertake. Other members of your Twelve Step group, or if you are in therapy, your therapist, can also serve as guides. Record on this page who your guides will be.

This workbook concludes with a set of suggested readings. The workbook also provides a format to supplement your guides, your reading, and if you have the companion tapes, your listening. A thoughtful approach on your part will enhance the workbook. Your guides will also make suggestions, especially about readings appropriate to your program.

MY GUIDES WILL BE:

Sponsor

_____

Others

_____

_____

_____

1

Step One

We admitted we were powerless over
our addiction,
that our lives had become
unmanageable.

The First Step requires an admission of powerlessness over living in the extremes. As part of this step, you assemble evidence to document both powerlessness and unmanageability in your life. This is the beginning of understanding the story of your illness. Clearly specifying the history becomes essential to the unfolding of the story. The following exercises will help you in documenting your history:

Family Tree and Addiction — Most addicts have other addicts and co-addicts in their families. By thinking through your family tree, some patterns may emerge that will show how some part of your powerlessness started within your family.

Addiction History — As an addict and/or co-addict, other addictions will have impacted on your powerlessness. One example would be the sex addict whose alcoholic behavior affected his sexual acting out. Another example would be the co-dependent whose excessive weight from compulsive overeating increased feelings of unworthiness.

Abuse Checklist — Sexual, physical and emotional abuse are common in addictive families. Children are powerless over the abuse they receive from the adults in their lives; also, the abuse damaged them in fundamental ways which serve as catalysts to their becoming addicted and co-addicted.

Step One for Addicts — Once you have documented your history in the above three exercises, you'll be ready to start working and reflecting on your First Step. You'll begin to carefully document the powerlessness and unmanageability in your own life.

Step One for Co-Addicts — You'll specify the type of addiction to which you are co-addicted, and document your powerlessness and unmanageability.

Note for all addicts: A high probability exists that you are co-addicted as well. At some point you may wish to return and do a First Step on your co-addiction.

Sharing Your First Step — Part of really taking a First Step is sharing what you've learned about your story with your guides and others in the program. Remember, the answers may not come easily as you complete the exercises. When you feel stuck, get your guides to help you!

FAMILY TREE AND ADDICTION

©1988 Patrick Carnes, Ph.D.

As part of Step One it is often helpful to understand "powerlessness" in terms of the family system. Diagram your family of origin back three generations. After entering each person's name, record any of the following characteristics by placing the number of the item next to the name. If you are unsure but have a good guess about an individual, simply put the number of your guess and circle it. Thus, if grandfather John Smith was a compulsive overeater and you think an alcoholic as well, you would enter *John Smith* (1, ④).

Compulsive or Addictive Characteristics:

1. alcoholic

2. compulsive gambler

3. anorexic/bulimic

4. compulsive overeater

5. sex addict

6. victim of child abuse

7. perpetrator of child abuse

8. mental health problem

9. other compulsive or addictive behavior (please label)

10. co-addict

FAMILY TREE AND ADDICTION (cont'd.)

©1988 Patrick Carnes, Ph.D.

father
grandfather
great-grandfather
great-grandmother
grandmother
great-grandfather
great-grandmother

mother
grandfather
great-grandfather
great-grandmother
grandmother
great-grandfather
great-grandmother

Now list any other relatives (brothers, sisters, uncles, aunts, cousins) who fit one of the ten categories. Example: Fred Smith (uncle) (1, ⑤).

1. _____
2. _____
3. _____
4. _____
5. _____
6. _____
7. _____
8. _____
9. _____
10. _____
11. _____
12. _____

Are there patterns of addiction in your family? What reflections do you now have about your own powerlessness given the role of addiction in your family? Can you see ways in which your addictive behavior was learned, or ways your behavior was a form of coping with an unhealthy family environment?

Record these reflections here:

ADDICTION HISTORY

©1988 Patrick Carnes, Ph.D.

As part of Step One, it helps to chronicle how various addictions or self-abusive behaviors have affected one another. Review the following categories of addictive or "unstoppable" behaviors. Simply write examples of how other out-of-control behaviors affected the development of your addiction or co-addiction during each age category. The notes can be short and descriptive.

Example: Compulsively masturbating at age 6 in order to sleep—was worst when Dad was drunk and violent—using sex to deal with my co-dependent fear.

Another example: My weight was heaviest at 29 when I was sexually acting out the worst.

Behavior	Age 0-10	Age 10-18	Age 18-25	Age 25-40	Age 40+
Eating					

ADDICTION HISTORY (cont'd.)

Behavior	Age 0-10	Age 10-18	Age 18-25	Age 25-40	Age 40+
Other examples of compulsive behavior (Give label, for example: shoplifting, spending, smoking, working, dangerous or high-risk behaviors.)					

ADDICTION HISTORY (cont'd.)

Behavior	Age 0-10	Age 10-18	Age 18-25	Age 25-40	Age 40+
Sexual					
Co-Addiction					

ADDICTION HISTORY (cont'd.)

Behavior	Age 0-10	Age 10-18	Age 18-25	Age 25-40	Age 40+
Gambling					
Alcohol					

Now that you have completed your addiction history, think about how your addictions and co-dependency affected one another. How does looking at the patterns of "extreme" living help you in looking at your First Step?

Record your reflections here:

NOTES

◼ ABUSE CHECKLIST

The following checklist and worksheet will help you assess the extent to which you were abused in your own childhood experience. Read over each of the three categories of abuse (sexual, physical, emotional). Fill in the information in the spaces next to the items which apply to you. For each type of abuse, record the information to the best of your memory.

AGE: How old were you when it started?

ABUSING PERSONS: Who abused you? Father, step-father, mother, stepmother, adult relative, adult friend, adult neighbor, professional person, brother or sister, or stranger?

FREQUENCY: How often did it happen? Daily, two to three times a week, weekly, monthly, or occasionally?

FORM OF ABUSE	AGE	ABUSING PERSON	FREQUENCY
A. SEXUAL ABUSE			
Suggestive flirting			
Propositioning			
Inappropriate holding, kissing			
Fondling of sexual parts			
Masturbation			
Oral sex			
Forced sexual activity			
Other			

THE ABUSE CHECKLIST (cont'd.)

FORM OF ABUSE	AGE	ABUSING PERSON	FREQUENCY
B. PHYSICAL ABUSE			
Scratching, pinching, shoving			
Slapping, punching, whipping			
Burns			
Cutting, wounding			
Broken bones, fractures			
Damage to organs			
Permanent injury			
Other			

THE ABUSE CHECKLIST (cont'd.)

FORM OF ABUSE	AGE	ABUSING PERSON	FREQUENCY
C. EMOTIONAL ABUSE			
Neglect			
Denigration of worth			
Harassment, malicious tricks			
Blackmail			
Unfair punishments			
Cruel or degrading tasks			
Cruel confinement			
Abandonment			
Other			

How did the abuse you received affect you as a child? How do you feel in reflecting on these events? What has been the impact on your addictive or co-addictive behavior?

Record your answers here:

Gentleness Break

You have just completed a significant piece of work. Congratulations! Before you continue with the First Step exercises, stop and reward yourself. Choose one of the following activities to be gentle with yourself. If none of these appeals to you, find one of your own. If you feel compelled to keep on working, remember you can become compulsive about the workbook, too. So...

Pet a warm puppy.

Play with a child.

Enjoy a long nap.

Make a cup of tea.

Walk with a friend.

Ask for a hug.

Do something not useful but fun.

Sit by a lake or a stream.

Work in a garden.

Meditate.

Listen to favorite music.

Talk with a friend.

Read a novel.

Watch the sun set.

Sit with a teddy bear.

Ask someone to nurture you.

STEP ONE FOR ADDICTS

> We admit we are powerless over
>
> _____
> (insert alcohol or sex, etc.)
> **and that our lives have become unmanageable.**

Acceptance of the First Step paves the way to recovery. As you grow to understand your own powerlessness and how unmanageable your life became when you tried to control your addiction, you begin to understand the power that addiction has had over your life. Acknowledging your powerlessness and recognizing the unmanageability in your life will help to prepare you to use the rest of the Twelve Steps.

Fill in the following chart for a clearer picture of your addiction. Either write your examples out in detail or say a word or two that will remind you of the situation. Sharing your First Step with your group or your guides will allow them to help you in your recovery. Doing the worksheet and keeping it to yourself will not help your recovery. (See Sharing Your First Step.) If one of the aspects of addiction does not apply to you, just leave it blank.

Aspect of Addiction	Give Three or More Examples
1. Obsessing or fantasizing about my addictive behavior?	_____ _____ _____ _____ _____

Aspect of Addiction	Give Three or More Examples
2. Trying to control my behavior?	
3. Lying, covering up, or minimizing my behavior?	
4. Trying to understand and/or rationalize my behavior?	
5. Effects on my physical health?	

Aspect of Addiction	Give Three or More Examples
6. Feeling guilty or shameful about my behaviors?	
7. Effects on my emotional health?	
8. Effects on my social life?	
9. Effects on my school or work life?	

Aspect of Addiction	Give Three or More Examples
10. Effects on my character, morals, or values?	_____ _____ _____ _____ _____
11. Effects on my spirituality?	_____ _____ _____ _____ _____
12. Effects on my financial situation?	_____ _____ _____ _____ _____
13. Contact with the police or courts?	_____ _____ _____ _____ _____

Aspect of Addiction	Give Three or More Examples

14. Has my preoccupation led to insane or strange behavior?

_____

_____

_____

_____

15. Has my preoccupation led to loss of memory?

_____

_____

_____

_____

16. Has my preoccupation led to destructive behavior against self or others?

_____

_____

_____

_____

17. Has my preoccupation led to accidents or other dangerous situations?

_____

_____

_____

_____

Aspect of Addiction	Give Three or More Examples
18. Do I keep overly or unnecessarily busy?	
19. Do I feel depressed a lot of the time?	
20. Am I able to share my feelings? If not, why?	
21. Have I changed my physical image to support my addiction?	

Aspect of Addiction	Give Three or More Examples
22. Have I made promises to myself that I have broken?	
23. Have I denied that I have a problem?	
24. Has my addiction affected my self-esteem?	
25. Have I tried to relieve my pain about my behavior? How?	

Aspect of Addiction	Give Three or More Examples
26. Have I tried to manipulate people into supporting my addiction? How?	
27. Have I given up my hobbies and interests? What were these?	

■ POWERLESSNESS INVENTORY

List as many examples as you can think of that show how powerless you have been to stop your behavior. Remember, "powerless" means unable to stop the behavior despite obvious consequences. Be very explicit about types of behavior and frequencies. Start with your earliest example of being powerless and conclude with your most recent. Generate at least thirty examples. Remember gentleness. You do not have to complete the list in one sitting. Add to the list as examples occur to you. By generating as many examples as possible, you will have added significantly to the depth of your understanding of your own powerlessness. When you finish this inventory do not proceed until you have discussed it with one of your guides. The gentle way means you deserve support with each piece of significant work.

Example: Sarah said she would leave in 1972 if I slipped again and I did it anyway.

1. _____

2. _____

3. _____

4. _____

5. _____

6. _____

7. _____

8. _____

9. _____

10. _____

11. _____

12. _____

13. _____

14. _____

15. _____

16. _____

17. _____

18. _____

19. _____

20. _____

21. _____

22. _____

23. _____

24. _____

25. _____

26. _____

27. _____

28. _____

29. _____

30. _____

UNMANAGEABILITY INVENTORY

List as many examples as you can think of that show how your life has become totally unmanageable because of your dependency. Remember, "unmanageability" means that your addiction created chaos and damage in your life. Again, when you finish this inventory, stop and talk to your guides. You deserve support.

Example: Got caught stealing in 1979 to support my addiction.

1. _____

2. _____

3. _____

4. _____

5. _____

6. _____

7. _____

8. _____

9. _____

10. _____

11. _____

12. _____

13. _____

14. _____

15. _____

16. _____

17. _____

18. _____

19. _____

20. _____

21. _____

22. _____

23. _____
    _____

24. _____
    _____

25. _____
    _____

26. _____
    _____

27. _____
    _____

28. _____
    _____

29. _____
    _____

30. _____
    _____

STEP ONE FOR CO-ADDICTS

> **We admit we are powerless over co-addiction to**
>
> _____
>
> (insert type of addiction)
>
> **and that our lives have become unmanageable.**

Acceptance of the First Step paves the way to recovery. When new to the Twelve Step program, most people find it easier to recognize the "sick" behavior of the addict than to recognize their own co-addictive behavior. As you grow to understand your own powerlessness and how unmanageable your life became when you tried to control the addiction, you begin to understand the power that addiction has had over your life. Acknowledging your powerlessness and recognizing your unmanageability will help to prepare you to use the rest of the Twelve Steps.

Fill in the following chart for a clearer picture of your co-addiction. Either write your examples out in detail or say a word or two that will remind you of the situation. Sharing your First Step with your group or your guides will allow them to help you in your recovery. If you have a hard time thinking of examples, ask them to help you. Doing the worksheet and keeping it to yourself will not help your recovery. (See Sharing Your First Step.) If one of the aspects of co-addiction does not apply to you, just leave it blank.

Aspect of Co-Addiction	Give Three or More Examples
1. Obsession about the addict's behavior?	
2. How do I try to control the addict's behavior?	
3. Lying, covering up, or minimizing the addict's behavior?	
4. Attempts to figure out the addict's behavior?	

Aspect of Co-Addiction	Give Three or More Examples
5. Effects on my physical health?	
6. Effects on my emotional health?	
7. Effects on my social life?	
8. Effects on my school or work life?	

Aspect of Co-Addiction	Give Three or More Examples
9. Effects on my character, morals, or values?	
10. Effects on my spirituality?	
11. Effects on my financial situation?	
12. Contact with the police or courts?	

Aspect of Co-Addiction	Give Three or More Examples

13. Has my preoccupation with the addict led to insane or strange behavior?

14. Has my preoccupation with the addict led to loss of memory?

15. Has my preoccupation with the addict led to destructive behavior against myself or others?

16. Has my preoccupation with the addict led to accidents or other dangerous situations?

Aspect of Co-Addiction	Give Three or More Examples
17. Have I checked through the addict's personal mail, journals, etc.?	
18. Do I dress to accommodate the addict's wishes?	
19. Do I lecture the addict for his/her problem?	
20. Do I punish the addict? How?	

Aspect of Co-Addiction	Give Three or More Examples

21. Do I blame myself
    for the addict's
    problem?

_____

_____

_____

_____

_____

22. Do I use sex to get
    what I want?

_____

_____

_____

_____

_____

23. Do I make excuses
    to not be sexual?

_____

_____

_____

_____

_____

24. Do I attempt to
    persuade the addict
    to take care of him/
    herself?

_____

_____

_____

_____

_____

Aspect of Co-Addiction	Give Three or More Examples

25. Am I overly
    responsible or
    irresponsible?

26. Do I keep overly
    busy?

27. Do I feel depressed
    a lot of the time?

28. Am I able to deal
    with my feelings?

Aspect of Co-Addiction	Give Three or More Examples
29. Have I changed my physical image to please/displease the addict?	
30. Have I believed I could or should change the addict?	
31. Have I believed the addict's promises?	
32. Have I denied the addiction?	

Aspect of Co-Addiction	Give Three or More Examples
33. Has the addiction affected my self-esteem?	
34. Do I try to relieve the addict's pain?	
35. Have I tried to manipulate the addict into changing?	
36. Have I given up my hobbies and interests?	

Aspect of Co-Addiction	Give Three or More Examples

37. Has fear of
    rejection kept me
    in the relationship?

38. Do I put the pieces
    back together after
    the addict creates
    chaos?

CO-ADDICT'S POWERLESSNESS INVENTORY

List as many examples as you can think of that show how powerless you have been to stop your behavior. Remember, "powerless" means unable to stop your behavior despite obvious negative consequences. Be very explicit about types of behavior and frequencies. Start with your earliest example of being powerless and conclude with your most recent. Generate at least thirty examples. Remember gentleness. You do not have to complete the list in one sitting. Add to the list as examples occur to you. By generating as many examples as possible, you will have added significantly to the depth of your understanding of your own powerlessness. When you finish this exercise do not proceed until you have discussed it with one of your guides. The gentle way means you deserve support with each piece of significant work.

Example: I threatened to leave home in 1972 and he/she still did not stop drinking.

1. _____

_____

2. _____

_____

3. _____

_____

4. _____

_____

5. _____

_____

6. _____

_____

7. _____

8. _____

9. _____

10. _____

11. _____

12. _____

13. _____

14. _____

15. _____

16. _____

17. _____

18. _____

19. _____

20. _____

_____

21. _____

_____

22. _____

_____

23. _____

_____

24. _____

_____

25. _____

_____

26. _____

_____

27. _____

_____

28. _____

_____

29. _____

_____

30. _____

_____

CO-ADDICT'S
UNMANAGEABILITY INVENTORY

List as many examples as you can think of that show how your life has become totally unmanageable because of your co-dependency. Remember, "unmanageability" means that your co-addiction created chaos and damage in your life. Again, when you finish, stop and talk to your guides. You deserve support.

Example: In 1980, I had to get an extra job to support us because of his/her addiction.

1. _____

   _____

2. _____

   _____

3. _____

   _____

4. _____

   _____

5. _____

   _____

6. _____

   _____

7. _____

   _____

8. _____

   _____

9. _____

   _____

10. _____

11. _____

12. _____

13. _____

14. _____

15. _____

16. _____

17. _____

18. _____

19. _____

20. _____

21. _____

22. _____

23. _____

24. _____

25. _____

26. _____

27. _____

28. _____

29. _____

30. _____

Sharing Your First Step

You have not fully taken your First Step unless you share it with others. When you share your First Step, usually with a group, focus on telling about the depth and pain of your powerlessness, not necessarily on telling your whole story. Choose incidents that are most moving to you. Get feedback and support from your guides about what to share. Remember, your goal is not to perform for others, but to help you see and accept your powerlessness. The more honest you are, the more relief you will feel.

The First Step invites you to share freely, holding little back. This is called "taking a step" and means a fundamental acknowledgment of the illness and a surrender to a different life. Some people go through the motions of a First Step without actually taking the step. They avoid the step by sharing examples of their powerlessness and unmanageability as if they were unrelated: they are detached from the impact of their illness. Taking the step means admitting clearly the patterns of the illness and sharing the feelings that accompany the realization that you have been out of control. Healing only occurs when the step goes past intellectual acceptance to emotional surrender.

Here's a comparison of some of the characteristics of "taking" versus "avoiding" a step:

TAKING A STEP	AVOIDING A STEP
Deliberate	Speedy
Thoughtful	Just reporting
Emotionally present	Emotionally absent
Feelings congruent with reality	Absence of feelings

Statements of ownership of feelings and responsibility for behavior	Blame, denial, projection
Events form patterns	Events seem isolated
Acceptance	Defensiveness
Acknowledge impact	Deny impact
Surrender to illness	Attempt to limit illness
See addiction as part of life	See addiction as something to be fixed

Be aware of the tendency to become detached when telling your story. Try to remain open to both your own feelings and the group with whom you are sharing.

There are many reasons why people avoid, sometimes indefinitely, taking their First Step. Read the following items and see if any apply to you:

— **Failure of courage:** To face an illness requires great courage. Some people are unable or unwilling to do it. If you find yourself thinking that you "don't really need to do anything" or that you can "handle it by yourself," find someone in the program to support you in your fearful moments.

— **Not witnessing a good First Step:** If you have never seen a First Step taken, you have no real model of what to do. Watch someone else take the First Step or ask your guide to talk to you about his or her First Step—how it was taken, what it meant.

— **Inadequate preparation:** If you have not carefully prepared and consulted with your guides—that is, if you haven't carefully examined your own story—do not proceed. A First Step is not something you can do hastily.

— **Denial of impact:** If you find yourself minimizing ("Things were not so bad") or wondering if you are making something out of nothing, it's time to go back over your story with your guides.

— **Acting out:** Actively holding on to some aspect of the addiction or co-addiction, even in some very small way, will interfere with taking your First Step. Remember, you will not feel better until you completely stop your compulsive behavior.

— **Holding on to a major secret:** Secrets most often involve shame, and shame will serve as a barrier to the self-acceptance necessary in taking a First Step. Share the secret with your guides or therapist before proceeding.

— **Distrust of group:** Having confidence in your group is necessary in order for you to take the risks for your First Step work. If you do not feel comfortable in the group, talk to your guides about your options.

— **Inadequate understanding of the Twelve Step program:** When you were brought into the program, someone explained how the steps work. Each step has a special purpose; all Twelve Steps taken in order will lead you to recovery. If you are still confused about the program, seek some help before attempting your step work.

The concept of the "addictive personality shift" will help you here. Addicts and co-addicts acknowledge that in their illness it seems like there are two people inside them: the real person who tries to live up to values and cares about people, and another person whose values and relationships are sacrificed to addictive obsession. This Jekyll-Hyde experience is very common. The addict within us all is, in the words of the "Big Book" of Alcoholics Anonymous, "cunning and baffling." Even being able to recognize the shift from when you are your true self and when your addict has taken over is an extremely helpful tool for detaching from your addict's power.

In terms of your First Step, your addict within will work hard to sabotage your efforts at an open sharing of your illness. List below five ways your addict might try to interfere with your First Step.

Example: Rationalization—"When I was drinking, my boss loved my work."

1. _____

_____

2. _____

_____

3. _____

_____

4. _____

_____

5. _____

_____

Sharing your step work is crucial throughout the program.

Guide Reactions

This page is reserved for comments from your guides about your progress on your First Step. It is a place where they can write their encouragement, support, and reactions. This, too, is part of your history. Completing this page and the other guide reaction pages in this workbook is optional, not a requirement. Remember, though, that part of recovery is learning to accept support and praise, and this is a good time to begin.

Guides write here:

Guide name: _____ Date: _____

The Serenity Prayer

No better statement of our need to reestablish balance in our lives can be found than in the Serenity Prayer.

God grant me the serenity...

Serenity means that I no longer recoil from the past, live in jeopardy because of my behavior now, or worry about the unknown future. I seek regular times to re-create myself and I avoid those times of depletion which make me vulnerable to despair and to old self-destructive patterns.

to accept the things I cannot change...

Accepting change means that I do not cause suffering for myself by clinging to that which no longer exists. All that I can count on is that nothing will be stable—except how I respond to the transforming cycles in my life of birth, growth, and death.

to change the things I can...

Which means remembering that to give up my attempts to control outcomes does not require I give up my boundaries or my best efforts. It does mean my most honest appraisal of the limits of what I can do.

and the wisdom to know the difference...

Wisdom becomes the never forgotten recognition of all those times when it seemed there was no way out, and new paths opened up like miracles in my life.

Reflection on the First Step

On this page and pages like it and the end of each chapter, you are asked to stop and summarize your feelings about the step you have just taken. It's important for you to appreciate the ground you have already covered, as well as to consider ways to keep from losing that ground.

Now that you have taken and shared your First Step, reflect on what it means to you. Reflect also on the Serenity Prayer. What things can you do to make the philosophy contained in this prayer part of your daily life?

Celebrating Your Progress

Congratulations on completing your First Step, so crucial to your recovery. If this step has left you open to shame attacks, you may want to spend a lot of time with people in the program who will help you stay on the gentle path. **Suggestion:** Create a celebration for yourself to mark your progress!

What are some of the gentle, healthy ways you can celebrate the new beginning you have made? What are some of the ways you can celebrate your progress as you work the program during the coming weeks and months?

Step Two

Came to believe
that a Power
greater than ourselves
could restore us to sanity.

Step Three

Made a decision
to turn our will and our lives
over to the care of God
as we understood Him.

The First Step asks you to admit that you have an illness. Steps Two and Three ask you to confront the question of what gives your life meaning. Without meaning in your life, your addictions and co-addictions can grow and thrive. Without meaning you cannot establish the priorities which help you restore the balance, focus, and self-responsibility you seek.

Ultimately, this question of meaning is a spiritual one. Steps Two and Three ask, Whom do you trust? Whom or what do you have faith in? How much you trust your Higher Power often parallels how you trust the people in your life. If you have trouble accepting help from others and insist on handling things alone, chances are you will resist the help of a Higher Power in your life. And many addicts who have worked the program realize that if they refuse help after admitting that they are powerless and damaged, they will remain stuck in their insanity.

Four things will make these steps easier:

Spiritual Care Inventory — Helps you identify obstacles to completing Step Two and Step Three.

Loss of Reality Inventory — Helps you focus on your priorities.

One Year to Live Fantasy — An exercise in confronting your own death. Provides perspective on the spirituality and meaningfulness of your life.

Letter to Your Higher Power — Gives you a concrete way to express your spiritual decisions.

Remember to include your guides in this process.

SPIRITUAL CARE INVENTORY

Your first task in the Spiritual Care Inventory is to pinpoint to what degree you are able to accept help from others and from a Higher Power. Begin by circling the six words that best describe you now:

beginning	rebellious	loner	cooperative
scared	challenging	unique	nurturing
uncertain	resisting	free	guiding
tentative	nontrusting	separate	assisting
learner	questioning	individualist	directing
vulnerable	testing	detached	reliable

Now circle the six words that best describe God, as you understand God or your Higher Power:

judgmental	caring	distant	hoax
strict	trustable	indifferent	unreal
negative	loving	uncaring	nonexistent
rigid	purposeful	nonattentive	fanciful
cruel	compassionate	absent	imaginary
arbitrary	predictable	disengaged	joke

As part of developing an identity, we all experience different phases of dependency (how much we depend on others for help). These phases can be defined as follows:

Dependence — we need and want help.

Counterdependence — we need help but resist it.

Independence — we are self-sufficient and do not need help.

Interdependence — we give/get help to and from others.

From the list of twenty-four words above, you were asked to select the six words which most aptly describe you. Now these same twenty-four words are arranged below in terms of dependence, counterdependence, independence, and interdependence. Find the six words you selected above and circle them again. Have you circled three or more words in any one category?

Dependence	Counterdependence	Independence	Interdependence
beginning	rebellious	loner	cooperative
scared	challenging	unique	nurturing
uncertain	resisting	free	guiding
tentative	nontrusting	separate	assisting
learner	questioning	individualist	directing
vulnerable	testing	detached	reliable

What patterns emerge in the words you selected? Do you see a connection between the words that describe you and the patterns of your addiction or co-addiction?

_____

_____

_____

_____

_____

Consider the following:

In a grocery store when searching for something you cannot find, do you (check one):

[ ] Keep searching until you find it.

[ ] Ask for help.

When putting something together from a kit, do you (check one):

[ ] Follow directions carefully.

[ ] Quickly go through the instructions only when you get stuck.

[   ] Figure it out yourself.

When you are personally in pain and need support, do you usually:

[   ] Talk to people immediately.

[   ] Wait until the crisis is over and then tell people.

[   ] Get through it the best way you can without help.

As you responded to these situations, did you discover a pattern of not letting yourself be helped? Often addicts and co-addicts rely on themselves.

As an addict and/or co-addict, you have relied on your obsessions to deal with pain and difficulty. You may have learned not to depend on people for help, care, and support. It is probable that you learned not to accept help based on the way your primary caregivers treated you as a child. Consider the following list of people. How did they affect your ability to receive help? Did they support you when you made a mistake? Did they show you how to do things or did they expect you to know already?

Your father _____

_____

_____

Your mother _____

_____

_____

Brothers and sisters _____

_____

_____

_____

_____

Other significant adults (specify) _____

_____

_____

_____

_____

_____

_____

_____

Teachers (specify)_____

_____

_____

_____

_____

_____

Employers (specify)_____

_____

_____

_____

Clergy (specify) _____

_____

_____

_____

Your perceptions of a Higher Power have evolved over the years. Before you can be truly reflective about a Higher Power, you need to clarify your attitudes toward God. Four types of God exist for many of us:

A punishing God who punishes our mistakes but does not reward or help.

An accepting God who accepts that we fail and cares anyway.

A noninvolved God who is detached and unconcerned with our lives.

A nonexistent God from whom no help is available.

These concepts often interfere with determining your relationship with your Higher Power.

Earlier from a list of twenty-four words you selected six words which most aptly described your perceptions of God. These twenty-four words are arranged below in terms of a punishing, accepting, noninvolved, or nonexistent God. Circle the six words you selected previously. Does any category get three or more words?

Punishing	Accepting	Noninvolved	Nonexistent
judgmental	caring	distant	hoax
strict	trustable	indifferent	unreal
negative	loving	uncaring	nonexistent
rigid	purposeful	nonattentive	fanciful
cruel	compassionate	absent	imaginary
arbitrary	predictable	disengaged	joke

Were there any patterns in the words you selected? Has your perception of God or Higher Power changed over time?

_____

_____

_____

_____

How does your current mode of accepting help (dependent, counter-dependent, independent, and interdependent) fit with your perception of God or Higher Power?

_____

_____

_____

_____

_____

Name the five persons who most influenced your attitudes toward God or Higher Power:

1. _____

2. _____

3. _____

4. _____

5. _____

Do they have anything in common? _____

_____

_____

What obstacles does your religious background/upbringing create for you in trusting a Higher Power?

_____

_____

_____

_____

_____

What strengths does your religious background/upbringing create for you in trusting a Higher Power?

_____

_____

_____

_____

_____

Based on what you have learned about recovery so far, how do you see the "turning over" process of Step Two? What are the things that might prevent you, emotionally and intellectually, from accepting the help of a Higher Power?

_____

_____

_____

_____

_____

_____

_____

_____

_____

_____

_____

_____

_____

_____

_____

_____

In what ways do you see a Higher Power working in your life now?

1. _____

_____

2. _____

_____

3. _____

_____

4. _____

_____

5. _____

_____

6. _____

_____

7. _____

_____

8. _____

_____

9. _____

_____

10. _____

_____

11. _____

_____

12. _____

_____

LOSS OF REALITY INVENTORY

Denial and delusion come from addictive and co-addictive impaired thinking. Considering that insanity involves some loss of touch with reality, addicts and co-addicts need to regain perspective on what is real and what is not. Here are three descriptive categories of reality loss:

1. **No reality**—Memory is lost due to a combination of factors including obsession, overextension, exhaustion, or anxiety and intoxication. Or, contact is lost with here-and-now events due to the same combination.

2. **Distortion of reality**—Reality is blurred because of the addiction's power. Think of things you thought were true because your addict wanted them to be. Or, the distortion of reality due to faulty beliefs. (If you start with a faulty belief, such as "women have to be seduced in order to enjoy sex," your thought processes will naturally be faulty as well, i.e., seduction is the only way to get needs met.)

3. **Ignoring reality**—The clear assessment of risks is set aside. Or, the recognition that recent experiences were disastrous is overcome by the compulsion to repeat them.

Now complete the Loss of Reality Inventory by reflecting on how you have lost contact with reality. Write specific examples under each of the following categories.

▶

No reality:

_____

_____

_____

_____

_____

_____

_____

_____

_____

Distortion of reality:

_____

_____

_____

_____

_____

_____

_____

_____

_____

_____

_____

Ignoring reality:

_____

_____

_____

_____

_____

_____

_____

_____

_____

_____

Now reflect on your losses of reality. When you needed help, whom did you ask? When you asked your Higher Power or other people for help, was your request based on reality?

_____

_____

_____

_____

_____

_____

_____

_____

_____

_____

THE ONE YEAR TO LIVE FANTASY

Reclaiming reality starts with a clear sense of our limitations as human beings. But we live in a culture that denies these limitations. We are constantly invited to overextend ourselves—for example, to spend more than we earn, work more than we need to, or eat more than we should. We live as if there were no end. We literally deny our own mortality.

A powerful exercise which can show you your own limitations is to picture your own death. Looking at death provides vital perspectives about what gives your life meaning, what priorities you are ignoring, and who your Higher Power is.

Set aside some uninterrupted time to experience this fantasy and answer the questions provided at the end. Make sure you are physically comfortable. If you do not have the accompanying audiotapes, you may read the fantasy, or have your guide or a close friend read it to you.

Fantasy:

Imagine you are in your physician's office. (What does it look, smell, and feel like?) Your doctor comes in and tells you that results from the tests are in. You have a terminal illness. All the other doctors consulted agree. They think you will maintain your physical ability for about a year—but at the end of the year you will die. (Reflect for a moment.)

Imagine your first reactions as you walk out of the office. What do you do? How do you spend those first few hours and days? Do you tell anyone? (Reflect.)

As you start to adjust to your dying, do you change your life? Stop work? Do something different? (Reflect.)

Maybe you want to do something different. Perhaps you wish to travel? Where would you go? Picture yourself traveling—whom would you bring with you? (Reflect.)

Perhaps you might want to do things you have never done before. Activities like skydiving, scuba diving, race car driving—things that seemed to be too dangerous before, but now it doesn't make any difference. What have you always wanted to do but been afraid to do? Picture yourself doing them. Who is with you? (Reflect.)

Almost all of us have "unfinished" parts of our lives: a book we are writing, a family room to finish, a family project like getting the family album in order for the kids. What unfinished projects would be important enough to finish before you die? Imagine yourself doing them. (Reflect.)

For some of us, the unfinished parts include things unsaid to others—like "I'm sorry" or "I love you." Picture yourself saying the things you would need to say before you die. (Reflect.)

It's now about three months before you die. You can start to feel your health fail. While you can still function, you decide to try one last thing. What would that be? What would be one of the last things you would want to do before you die? Who is with you? (Reflect.)

It's now a matter of weeks before you die. Where do you go to die? Your home? A family farm? A lake? The mountains? The city? (Reflect.) How do you spend those last days? Who is with you? (Reflect.)

As you think over the events of this last year of your life, what were the most significant for you? (Reflect.) In fact, think of these and all the events of your life—which stand out now as the things that made it worthwhile? (Reflect.) And as you reflect on these events, be aware that you are working on this workbook. And you are very much alive.

About the fantasy. . .

Often this fantasy helps people touch their own grief about losses in their lives. If you feel sad, do not avoid the feelings. Rather, use them and let them support you in coming to terms with the losses. Sharing the fantasy and your feelings with your guides can deepen your understanding of the issues the fantasy raises. First, record the details of your fantasy in the space provided. Then answer the questions that follow.

Your first reactions: _____

_____

_____

_____

_____

_____

Changes you would make in your life: _____

_____

_____

_____

_____

New things you would try: _____

_____

_____

_____

_____

Unfinished things you want to complete: _____

_____

_____

_____

_____

_____

Things you need to say before you die: _____

_____

_____

_____

_____

_____

Describe your last fling: _____

_____

_____

_____

_____

Spiritual preparations: _____

_____

_____

_____

_____

_____

Where and how you would spend your last days: _____

_____

_____

_____

_____

_____

_____

Throughout the fantasy there were key moments to involve significant persons in your life. Whom did you involve and what did you learn about your relationship priorities?

_____

_____

_____

_____

_____

_____

If during the fantasy you found yourself doing things significantly different from how you live now, why? If they were so important to get done, what prevents you from doing them now?

_____

_____

_____

_____

_____

_____

How do you feel about facing your own death?

_____

_____

_____

_____

_____

Thinking about death provides a way to look at what is real and what is important in our lives. Delusion, balance, focus, self-responsibility, dependency, meaning—all that addicts and co-addicts wrestle with—are seen in a new light. Go back to the Loss of Reality Inventory. How do you view your denial and delusion when you reflect on your own death?

_____

_____

_____

_____

_____

_____

_____

_____

_____

_____

_____

_____

_____

_____

_____

_____

_____

_____

_____

_____

_____

_____

_____

Gentleness Break

Before proceeding with your letter to your Higher Power, take a gentleness break. You have already accomplished so much and you need some time to look at your learnings before going on. Here are some suggestions:

Read a story to a child.

Rediscover the fun of doodling with
colored pencils or crayons.

Try a crossword puzzle.

Paddle a canoe.

Walk by a lake or stream.

Smell a flower.

Watch some birds.

Go sit in a church.

Invite a friend to take you out to dinner.

Get a massage.

Run, swim, or bike.

From this point on, there will be no more scheduled gentleness breaks. It's up to you to pace yourself and to determine when to take a break and how to spend that gentle time.

▛ LETTER TO YOUR HIGHER POWER

The Second and Third Steps become very concrete when you write a letter to your Higher Power. By writing the letter, you make your belief and trust into an active process. You will find it helpful to include in your letter how you "came to believe" and what the "decision" to turn over your will and your life means to you. Be specific about what you are turning over. Remember the Second and Third Steps are acts of confidence or faith.

People use many different names in addressing their Higher Power, but what seems to work the best is when you make it as personal as possible.

When you have written the letter, read it out loud to your guide. We need to share our spiritual experiences with others in order to make sense out of them.

Dear _____ ,

_____

_____

_____

_____

_____

_____

_____

_____

_____

_____

Trusting life comes from making some meaning of
who we are, what we are all about.
When we confront shame, we become aware of
emptiness, a spiritual hunger.
Our attempts to fill this hunger with controlling,
compulsive behaviors only lead to pain and
remorse. Carl Jung was aware of this compulsive
"filling of the void." He wrote to Bill Wilson, the
co-founder of AA, saying that he thought
alcoholism was the search for wholeness, for a
"union with God."

— Merle A. Fossum & Marilyn J. Mason
Facing Shame: Families in Recovery

Reflect on the Fossum/Mason quote above and how you feel about the
Second and Third Steps in your life.

The Second and Third Steps are very personal transactions and create a special intimacy when shared with others in the program. Have your guides who have shared in your process record their personal reactions here.

Guides: What expressions of trust or faith do you have in the work the owner of this workbook has done?

Guide name: _____ Date: _____

NOTES

Guide name: _____ Date: _____

Step Four

Made a searching and
fearless moral
inventory of our
ourselves.

Step Five

Admitted to God,
to ourselves,
and to another human being
the exact nature of our wrongs.

With the First Step you admitted your powerlessness and vulnerability. The Second and Third Steps helped you gain the support you need from your Higher Power and other people to face the reality of addiction and co-addiction in your life. With that support you can make a fearless moral inventory and use it to examine the damage your illness has caused. This thorough self-assessment will impel you to let go of much of what keeps you in your compulsive patterns. Recovery requires giving up the old ways—ways in which you nurtured yourself by living in the extremes. In that sense, the Fourth and Fifth Steps are a grieving process. The feelings that go into the grieving process in the Fourth and Fifth Steps include discomfort, anger, fear, shame, sadness, and loneliness. Discomfort is the outer layer of feelings, anger the second layer, and so on down to the inner-most feeling of loneliness.

These feelings, which are layers of your internal self, serve as a barometer of how you feel about your behavior. They can also be a structure on which you build your moral inventory.

You will find the Fourth Step inventory to be a deeply personal experience with each layer guiding you to a deeper relationship with yourself.

Notice, however, that the innermost layer is loneliness, in which you confront the existential reality of your aloneness and estrangement. However, the program, in its wisdom, asks you in the Fifth Step to find and share with another person the work you have done on your Fourth Step. You do not need to be alone. The program builds in more support for you at each difficult turn in your path.

The person you select to hear your Fourth Step can be someone in the program, a sponsor, or a member of the clergy. In addition to being deeply personal, the Fourth and Fifth steps are spiritual experiences.

Before starting on your Fourth Step, set a time with the person who will hear your Fifth Step. There are several reasons for this. First, the Fourth Step is an awesome task and easy to put off. By making an appointment you make a commitment to get the task done. Even if you have to reset the appointment, the focus will be on getting the step done. Second, the person who will hear your Fifth Step may have some suggestions for you to help you in your process. Finally, you will know for sure that someone will be there for you when the path becomes difficult and painful. Again, do not forget to involve your other guides in the process as well. You do the task yourself, but you do not have to be alone. Each section will generate feelings. You do not have to wait to share them. Talk about them as they stir, not after you have figured them out.

Within each layer of feelings you will find elements of your moral inventory that are good and positive as well as negative. As you survey the wreckage caused by your illness, you may assume that a Fourth Step focuses on all the failures, mistakes, and harm done. However, to restore integrity means to claim the successes, the goodness, the courage, and the effort as well.

Sometimes when things seem dark it is difficult to claim the positive in your life. If it is difficult to take credit for positive things in yourself, look at it this way. In your addiction, you probably worked hard to cover the dark side of yourself, and showed only the good parts to the world. You lived between the secrets, shame, exploitation and abuse of your hidden addict and the care, responsibility and values of the public you. You probably even felt phony about your public self, because people did not know the real you behind the image you showed to the world. When you face the addict within you in the Fourth Step, your addiction becomes your teacher about the goodness in you. Ask yourself, Was your addict strong? enduring? clever? willing to risk? resourceful? All these are qualities of yourself that your addict borrowed upon to become powerful. They are equally available to you in your recovery.

Unfortunately, many people attempt a recovery by doing the opposite of what they did in their active illness: they focus only on the bad side and bury the good. The Fourth Step presents an opportunity for you to reclaim those good parts of yourself and use them for your recovery. A difficult challenge, to be sure, but the result is that you get to be the real you. You don't have to have an addictive, dark side draining all your power in its secrecy. And you don't have to feel phony or insincere when you own all parts of yourself. Besides, it is much easier to face your recovery secure in the knowledge of the good things you do have to draw upon. It is the more gentle way.

The Fourth Step is a demanding and even draining experience. Pace yourself. Take several gentleness breaks. This is hard and important work and you can take the time it deserves.

Now, proceed to your first Fourth Step inventory.

FOURTH STEP INVENTORY:
Avoiding Personal Responsibility

When taking Step Four, the first feeling you get in touch with is often discomfort. When people get uncomfortable about their behavior—especially where the potential of real pain is involved—they look for ways to protect themselves from the consequences of that behavior. Some of these ways are dysfunctional and self-destructive. These defensive manipulations serve to avoid responsibility. Examples include blaming others, denial, dishonesty, intimidation, and rationalization. Sometimes you may even go to great lengths to make people in your life feel crazy by pretending realities exist that do not. Or you take actions which distract or divert attention from your behavior. **How have you avoided taking responsibility for your behavior?** Give specific examples.

Example: Pretended Bill never told me about our appointment at school when really I forgot.

1. _____

2. _____

3. _____

4. _____

5. _____

6. _____

7. _____

8. _____

9. _____

10. _____

11. _____

12. _____

13. _____

14. _____

15. _____

16. _____

17. _____

18. _____

19. _____

20. _____

FOURTH STEP INVENTORY:
Taking Personal Responsibility

Sometimes you take responsibility for your discomfort. You can, for example, set boundaries about what you wish to talk about. Or you can express your discomfort and take responsibility for your behavior. **In what ways have you clearly owned your behavior?** Give specific examples.

Example: Admitted to Susan that I forgot our anniversary.

1. _____

_____

2. _____

_____

3. _____

_____

4. _____

_____

5. _____

_____

6. _____

_____

7. _____

_____

8. _____

_____

9. _____

_____

10. _____

_____

11. _____

_____

12. _____

_____

13. _____

_____

14. _____

_____

15. _____

_____

16. _____

_____

17. _____

_____

18. _____

_____

19. _____

_____

20. _____

_____

FOURTH STEP INVENTORY:
Misuse of Anger

Behind your defensive behavior there is a layer of anger. Perhaps you are angry because you got caught. Perhaps you are angry because you think people will leave you because of your behavior. You nurse grudges and resentments because you do not wish to admit the damage you have done. At times you may hold on to anger so that you can stay connected to others you don't want to lose emotionally. Sometimes you might use anger to justify your addiction. **In what ways have you misused your anger?** Give specific examples.

Example: Used resentment toward my spouse to justify an affair.

1. _____

   _____

2. _____

   _____

3. _____

   _____

4. _____

   _____

5. _____

   _____

6. _____

   _____

7. _____

   _____

8. _____

   _____

9. _____

10. _____

11. _____

12. _____

13. _____

14. _____

15. _____

16. _____

17. _____

18. _____

19. _____

20. _____

FOURTH STEP INVENTORY:
Positive Expression of Anger

Anger empowers people to resist manipulation and exploitation. Anger can give respect and dignity in abusive situations. Within an intimate relationship, anger is inevitable. Expressing the anger becomes an act of trust that the other person is important and capable of handling the anger. No relationship can survive without appropriate anger. **In what ways have you been respectful and assertive with your anger?** Give specific examples.

Example: I got angry with my alcoholic father when he started being cruel to my children.

1. _____

_____

2. _____

_____

3. _____

_____

4. _____

_____

5. _____

_____

6. _____

_____

7. _____

_____

8. _____

_____

9. _____

   _____

10. _____

   _____

11. _____

   _____

12. _____

   _____

13. _____

   _____

14. _____

   _____

15. _____

   _____

16. _____

   _____

17. _____

   _____

18. _____

   _____

19. _____

   _____

20. _____

   _____

FOURTH STEP INVENTORY:
Paralyzed by Fear

Fear is the next layer of feelings. Fear can be immobilizing. When did you need to take action but did not? Make yourself vulnerable but did not? Take a risk but did not? Have you put off important tasks and discussions? **In what ways have you compromised yourself by being stuck in your fear?** Give specific examples.

Example: I was afraid to admit how threatened I was about leaving my job—so no one understood.

1. _____

_____

2. _____

_____

3. _____

_____

4. _____

_____

5. _____

_____

6. _____

_____

7. _____

_____

8. _____

_____

9. _____

_____

10. _____

_____

11. _____

_____

12. _____

_____

13. _____

_____

14. _____

_____

15. _____

_____

16. _____

_____

17. _____

_____

18. _____

_____

19. _____

_____

20. _____

_____

■ FOURTH STEP INVENTORY:
Respect for Fear

Fear serves as an important guide for your safety. Sometimes it helps you to avoid disasters and take care of yourself. **When have you listened to your fear appropriately?** Give specific examples.

Example: I knew it was not a good idea to date the guy I met at the airport in the shape I was in.

1. _____

_____

2. _____

_____

3. _____

_____

4. _____

_____

5. _____

_____

6. _____

_____

7. _____

_____

8. _____

_____

9. _____

_____

10. _____

_____

11. _____

12. _____

13. _____

14. _____

15. _____

16. _____

17. _____

18. _____

19. _____

20. _____

FOURTH STEP INVENTORY:
Taking Healthy Risks

Moments occur in which you have to set your fears aside and take significant risks. **What risks have you taken for your own growth?** Give specific examples.

Example: I had an idea about a new business and took the risk to try it.

1. _____

_____

2. _____

_____

3. _____

_____

4. _____

_____

5. _____

_____

6. _____

_____

7. _____

_____

8. _____

_____

9. _____

_____

10. _____

_____

11. _____

_____

12. _____

_____

13. _____

_____

14. _____

_____

15. _____

_____

16. _____

_____

17. _____

_____

18. _____

_____

19. _____

_____

20. _____

_____

FOURTH STEP INVENTORY:
Shameful Events

At an even deeper layer, addicts feel shame. Without knowing your shadow side, you lose sight of your human limits. You need to know where you have not lived up to your values or when you have failed to practice what you preach. (Since you tell yourself that other people do not do what you did, you believe that if they found out you would be rejected.) You feel fundamentally embarrassed about yourself and feel unlovable. And the more shameful you feel, the more secretive you are.

A more realistic—and gentler—way of looking at your failures is to see that you are a limited human being who makes mistakes, who is lovable, and who is forgivable. You must also remember the powerlessness and unmanageability of your illness. With these things in mind, **in what ways have you not lived up to your own values?** (Suggestion: a good guideline is to start with a list of the things you have kept secret—these are at the core of shame.) Remember, be specific.

Example: A major secret I have is…or I feel really bad about…

1. _____

    _____

2. _____

    _____

3. _____

    _____

4. _____

    _____

5. _____

    _____

6. _____

    _____

7. _____

_____

8. _____

_____

9. _____

_____

10. _____

_____

11. _____

_____

12. _____

_____

13. _____

_____

14. _____

_____

15. _____

_____

16. _____

_____

17. _____

_____

18. _____

_____

19. _____

_____

20. _____

_____

FOURTH STEP INVENTORY: Pride in Your Achievements

As a balance, you need to account also for your achievements. Think of those moments when you lived up to your values or followed through on what you said you would do. Don't forget those times when you were courageous, generous, and exceeded your expectations. List those times when you were intimate, vulnerable, and caring. Don't forget to include your entry into your recovery program and getting this far in the workbook! **In what do you take pride?** Give specific examples.

Example: I feel good about how I supported my son when he was hurt last fall.

1. _____

_____

2. _____

_____

3. _____

_____

4. _____

_____

5. _____

_____

6. _____

_____

7. _____

_____

8. _____

_____

9. _____

_____

10. _____

_____

11. _____

_____

12. _____

_____

13. _____

_____

14. _____

_____

15. _____

_____

16. _____

_____

17. _____

_____

18. _____

_____

19. _____

_____

20. _____

_____

FOURTH STEP INVENTORY:
Losses and Painful Events

Beneath shame, there is often a feeling of sadness. Many variations of sadness exist for anyone who has lived with addictive extremes. First, you grieve for all the losses—time, people, opportunities, and dreams. Second, your sorrow for those you have harmed may be quite overwhelming. Finally, there is your pain about how deeply you have been hurt by this illness. **In what ways are you sad?** Give specific examples in each category.

Specific losses I feel:

Example: I am sorry about all the times I missed being with my children.

1. _____

_____

2. _____

_____

3. _____

_____

4. _____

_____

5. _____

_____

6. _____

_____

7. _____

_____

8. _____

_____

9. _____

_____

10. _____

_____

I have pain about these events:

Example: I hurt because of my teacher's abuse of me.

1. _____

_____

2. _____

_____

3. _____

_____

4. _____

_____

5. _____

_____

6. _____

_____

7. _____

_____

8. _____

_____

9. _____

_____

10. _____

_____

FOURTH STEP INVENTORY: Learning from Sadness

An old Buddhist saying suggests that suffering is clinging to that which changes. Grief, sorrow, and pain simply are part of life—especially given the powerlessness of your illness and your commitment to recovery. When you work through the feelings, they remain with you, and add depth to who you are. You integrate new learnings. Despite the losses, your life is better than before. **What gains have you made through your sadness?** Give specific examples.

Example: I have learned how to let people I love fail.

1. _____

_____

2. _____

_____

3. _____

_____

4. _____

_____

5. _____

_____

6. _____

_____

7. _____

_____

8. _____

_____

9. _____

_____

10. _____

_____

11. _____

_____

12. _____

_____

13. _____

_____

14. _____

_____

15. _____

_____

16. _____

_____

17. _____

_____

18. _____

_____

19. _____

_____

20. _____

_____

FOURTH STEP INVENTORY:
Beliefs about Your Unworthiness

The final feeling you will reach through your Fourth Step is that of loneliness. Addicts and co-addicts have lost the most important relationship of all—the relationship with oneself. How you treat yourself becomes the lens through which you view others. Fidelity to oneself results in faithfulness to others. Integrity with oneself generates trust of others. At our core, we are alone. So each of us needs to learn to enjoy ourselves, love ourselves, trust ourselves, and care for ourselves.

A word of caution: This final layer will be the hardest of all to be honest about. You will find all kinds of ways to resist doing this last part thoroughly. Since your relationship with yourself is the foundation of your recovery, take time to face this part of the inventory squarely.

You need to list beliefs you have about your own unworthiness—that is, about being a "bad" person. Seeing oneself as a flawed human being is core to the belief system of all addicts and co-addicts. Some of these faulty beliefs are easily identified as not true. Others are harder to contest. List all of them you can think of.

Example: I am a deceptive person.

1. _____

    _____

2. _____

    _____

3. _____

    _____

4. _____

    _____

5. _____

6. _____

7. _____

8. _____

9. _____

10. _____

11. _____

12. _____

13. _____

14. _____

15. _____

FOURTH STEP INVENTORY: Self-Hatred

After listing the beliefs you hold about your unworthiness, you need to be as explicit as possible about how deep the roots of your self-hatred go. As an addict, you have become an expert at beating yourself up. What things are you hardest on yourself about? **Make a list of examples of your self-hatred, including ways you have punished yourself, hurt yourself, put yourself down, or sold yourself out.** Do not forget to include fantasies of terrible things happening to you because you somehow "deserve" it.

Example: I take projects almost to the end and don't finish them.

1. _____

_____

2. _____

_____

3. _____

_____

4. _____

_____

5. _____

_____

6. _____

_____

7. _____

_____

8. _____

_____

9. _____

_____

10. _____

_____

11. _____

_____

12. _____

_____

13. _____

_____

14. _____

_____

15. _____

_____

16. _____

_____

17. _____

_____

18. _____

_____

19. _____

_____

20. _____

_____

FOURTH STEP INVENTORY:
Self-Affirmations

An affirmation is a statement about some goodness in you. **Spend some time thinking about the many positive qualities you possess.** How are you enjoyable, loving, caring, and trustable? This may be the most difficult of all your Fourth Step tasks. Sometimes early in recovery good things are more evident to others than they are to you. Ask for help. When you have completed your list, you might want to read it into a tape recorder. You will have a ready-made series of affirmations when you need them.

Example: I am a person of great courage.

1. I am _____

2. I am _____

3. I am _____

4. I am _____

5. I am _____

6. I am _____

7. I am _____

8. I am _____

9. I am _____

10. I am _____

11. I am _____

12. I am _____

13. I am _____

14. I am _____

15. I am _____

16. I am _____

17. I am _____

18. I am _____

19. I am _____

20. I am _____

21. I am _____

22. I am _____

23. I am _____

24. I am _____

25. I am _____

26. I am _____

27. I am _____

28. I am _____

29. I am _____

30. I am _____

The difficult road is the road of conversion,
the conversion from loneliness into solitude.
Instead of running away from our loneliness
and trying to forget or deny it,
we have to protect it and turn it into
a fruitful solitude.
To live a spiritual life we must first find the
courage to enter into the desert of our loneliness
and to change it by gentle and persistent efforts
into a garden of solitude.
This requires not only courage,
but also a strong faith.
As hard as it is to believe that the dry, desolate
desert can yield endless varieties of flowers,
it is equally hard to imagine that our loneliness
is hiding unknown beauty.
The movement from loneliness to solitude,
however, is the beginning of any spiritual life
because it is the movement from
the restless senses to the restful spirit,
from the outward-reaching cravings
to the inward-reaching search,
from the fearful clinging
to the fearless play.

— Henri Nouwen
Reaching Out

Read the words of Henri Nouwen above and reflect on the process of going through the layers of your Fourth Step. Record here your reactions to facing your own loneliness.

▶

STEP FIVE'S SHARING:
Suggestions for the Turning Point

Successful Fifth Steps come from sharing your written inventory with another person who will recognize and note the sources of greatest feeling or the places you were stuck. A consultant as well as a witness, the person who hears your Fifth Step will help you over the difficult parts of your story.

Remember also that the whole Fifth Step does not have to be done in one session. Some people who listen to Fifth Steps regularly recommend two to three sessions as opposed to a marathon event in which you share all your work at one time. Don't forget the gentleness of the path you are on.

Addicts and co-addicts often say that completing the Fifth Step was a real turning point in their recovery, that the first three steps took on new meaning, and that they felt anchored in the program. The Fifth Step does provide special support in the person who hears your story at perhaps the most difficult point in the program. The loneliness of the Fourth Step becomes an opportunity for reaching out. A special intimacy occurs when someone accepts you even though they know the very worst things about you. That experience of closeness can be duplicated as you deepen bonds with others in your life.

Spaces are provided on the following pages for you and the person you have shared your Fifth Step with to record your reactions, your feelings, and the progress you have made. Have fun with it together.

My feelings in sharing my Fifth Step:

_____

_____

_____

_____

_____

_____

_____

_____

_____

_____

_____

_____

_____

_____

_____

_____

_____

_____

_____

_____

_____

_____

Signed _____

Date _____

My feelings in hearing your Fifth Step:

_____

_____

_____

_____

_____

_____

_____

_____

_____

_____

_____

_____

_____

_____

_____

_____

_____

_____

_____

_____

_____

Signed _____

Date _____

It strikes us when, year after year,
the longed for perfection of life does not appear,
when the old compulsions reign within us
as they have for decades,
when despair destroys all joy and courage.
Sometimes at that moment a wave of light breaks
through our darkness, and it is as though a voice
were saying, "You are accepted."
YOU ARE ACCEPTED,
accepted by that which is greater than you
and the name of which you do not know.
Do not ask for the name now,
perhaps you will know it later.
Do not try to do anything,
perhaps later you will do much.
Do not seek for anything,
do not perform anything,
do not intend anything,
SIMPLY ACCEPT THE FACT
YOU ARE ACCEPTED.

— Paul Tillich

Read the Tillich quote above and reflect on the acceptance you experienced doing your Fifth Step. Record your thoughts and feelings here:

Step Six

Were entirely ready
to have God
remove all these
defects of character.

Step Seven

Humbly
asked Him
to remove
our shortcomings.

The Fourth and Fifth Steps revealed two types of shortcomings. The first are "defects" which were originally learned as survival tools. Many of your defenses were developed as a way to cope with growing up. For example, isolation may have been the only way to cope with abuse in your family. Now that you are in recovery, you can discard dysfunctional ways of taking care of yourself. You can embrace new healthy ways. In that sense, this stage of recovery parallels giving birth—a wondrous, painful, and at times ugly process.

One thing that can stop this process is relapse—which brings us to the other type of shortcomings, the "friends" of the addict within. These friends of the addict are grandiosity, pride, willfulness, jealousy, depression, suicidal preoccupation—all of those aspects of yourself which combine to make you vulnerable to your addiction and co-addiction. These are the shortcomings which can return you to the compulsive spirals you were in before you entered the program. Some of these shortcomings may have helped you survive in the past, but now they are a gateway to disaster.

Two tasks can help with the Sixth and Seventh Steps. First, make a list of those shortcomings you are willing to turn over to your Higher Power. Also list what you wish to put in place of your shortcomings. In other words, make a positive statement out of what you are turning over. For example, if dishonesty is your shortcoming, honesty is what you want. Then compose a meditation or prayer to help you remember that your Higher Power can help in this process.

Another task is to fill out a Personal Craziness Index (PCI, pronounced "picky"), a playful tool with a serious intent—to prevent relapse. The leading cause of relapse is lifestyle imbalance—being overstretched or overextended. At these times the "friends" of the addict within are immediately available.

Lifestyle imbalance makes the addict vulnerable to relapse in the following ways:

Feelings of entitlement: When overextended, addicts and co-addicts seek addictive nurturing because they are so depleted. They tell themselves they are entitled and "deserve" it, rationalizing the return to self-destructive patterns.

Increase of cravings: Urges to repeat the old cycles multiply when there has not been enough time to take care of oneself. Obsessional thinking is a relief to current stress.

Return of denial: In periods of imbalance, euphoric recall makes old cycles seem attractive again. Delusional thinking avoids the probable consequences of a return to previous behavior.

Reduction of coping ability: Overextension diminishes your ability to cope with problems. Bad decisions and poor problem solving further compound the crises in an unmanageable life.

Participation in high risk behaviors: Boundaries around critical situations, persons, and events which are normally avoided become elastic under stress. The reality of unsafe behavior becomes distorted by the overextension.

When you were in high school or college, you may have participated in an athletic program. Preparing for the stress of competition is called training. An athlete prepares for a stressful event (a match, game or tournament) by observing a training program that creates extra margins of endurance and strength and that develops skills for the event. Similarly, for an addict or a co-addict to participate in a recovery program is literally to be in training. You know that you are going to experience stress. You must prepare for that. Besides the skills you learn in your Twelve Step program, central to your training is a lifestyle that builds up reserves of strength and endurance.

Think of your life as having an addiction "set point"—the point where the imbalance leaves you vulnerable to addiction, when you are too stressed or overextended to maintain your recovery.

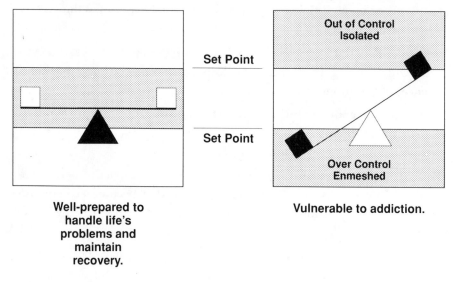

Lifestyle Balance

Set Point

Set Point

Well-prepared to
handle life's
problems and
maintain
recovery.

Lifestyle Imbalance

Out of Control
Isolated

Over Control
Enmeshed

Vulnerable to addiction.

By developing a sense of what your own personal set point is, you can be alert to maintaining the balance which makes you less vulnerable to the friends of your addict. The PCI on page 149 will help you develop some criteria for recognizing when you have passed that point of sanity and are at risk. The PCI thus can become a set of "training" guidelines under which you train for anticipated stress. In addition, by keeping track of your own PCI for a period of time, you will get better and better at maintaining lifestyle balance. And have some fun. First, on the next page list your defects of character and the qualities you will strive to develop.

STEP SIX:
Removing Character Defects

List below your character defects or shortcomings as you see them. As you list one, focus on the positive it can become and list that positive quality in the parallel column.

Shortcomings I am willing to turn over.

Qualities I wish to work towards.

Example: dishonesty

Example: honesty

1. _____	1. _____
2. _____	2. _____
3. _____	3. _____
4. _____	4. _____
5. _____	5. _____
6. _____	6. _____
7. _____	7. _____
8. _____	8. _____
9. _____	9. _____
10. _____	10. _____
11. _____	11. _____
12. _____	12. _____
13. _____	13. _____
14. _____	14. _____
15. _____	15. _____

SEVENTH STEP MEDITATION

Reflecting on your shortcomings, compose a prayer or meditation that you can use in times of stress to ask for help with your shortcomings. Suggestion: include reminders of how desperate you were in your addiction, of your commitment to recovery, and of your powerlessness.

PERSONAL CRAZINESS INDEX
Part One–Preparation

The Personal Craziness Index (PCI) is based on two assumptions:
1) craziness first appears in routine, simple behaviors which support lifestyle balance, and 2) behavioral signs will occur in patterns involving different parts of our lives. Thus, we can be caught up in issues of cosmic importance and not notice that our checking account is overdrawn. If our checking account is overdrawn, we are probably out of socks as well because we have not done our laundry. If this pattern is pervasive, there is risk that our lives will become emotionally bankrupt as well—cosmic issues notwithstanding.

Addicts and co-addicts are particularly vulnerable to the "insanity" of loss of reality due to neglecting the basics. "Keep it simple" and "a day at a time" are not shopworn cliches but guidelines borne out by the experience of many recovering people. The PCI helps as a reminder each day of what you need to do. It helps you establish good recovery habits. Without a process for such reminders, "cunning and baffling" self-destructive behavior returns. You'll also find the PCI helpful during periods of stress and vulnerability.

The process of creating your own PCI is designed to be as value-free as possible. Each person uses the index by setting his or her own criteria. In other words, generate behavioral signs (or as they are termed, "critical incidents") which, through your own experience, you have learned to be danger signs or warnings that you are "losing it," "getting out of hand," or "burnt out." Thus, you will judge yourself by your own standards.

You may change the items in the index as you progress in your recovery. The following are ten areas of personal behavior suggested as sources of danger signs. Please add some of your own if you wish.

1. **Physical Health**—The ultimate insanity is to not take care of your body. Without our bodies, we have nothing, yet we seem to have little time for physical conditioning. Examples are being overweight, cigarette or caffeine abuse, no regular exercise, eating junk food, insufficient sleep, lingering sickness. When do you know that you are not taking care of your body? (at least three examples):

   _____

   _____

   _____

2. **Transportation**—How people get from place to place is often a statement about their lifestyles. Take, for example, a car owner who seldom comes to a full stop, routinely exceeds the speed limit, runs out of gas, does not check the oil, puts off needed repairs, has not cleaned the back seat out in three months, and averages three speeding tickets and ten parking tickets a year. Or the bus rider who always misses the bus, never has change, forgets his or her briefcase on the bus, etc. What are the transportation behaviors that indicate your life is getting out of control? (at least three examples):

   _____

   _____

   _____

3. **Environment**—To not have time to do your personal chores is a comment on the order of your life. Consider the home in which plants go unwatered, fish unfed, grocery supplies depleted, laundry not done or put away, cleaning neglected, dishes unwashed, etc. What are ways in which you neglect your home or living space? (at least three examples):

   _____

   _____

   _____

4. **Work**—Chaos at work is risky for recovery. Signs of chaotic behavior are phone calls not returned in twenty-four hours, chronic lateness for appointments, being behind in promised work, an unmanageable in-basket, and "too many irons in the fire." When your life is unmanageable at work, what are your behaviors? (at least three examples):

_____

_____

_____

5. **Interests**—What are some positive interests besides work which give you perspective on the world? Music, reading, photography, fishing, or gardening are examples. What are you not doing when you are overextended? (at least three examples):

_____

_____

_____

6. **Social Life**—Think of friends in your social network who constitute significant support for you and are not family or significant others. When you become isolated, alienated or disconnected from them, what behaviors are typical of you? (at least three examples):

_____

_____

_____

7. **Family/Significant Others**—When you are disconnected from those closest to you, what is your behavior like? Examples are silent, overtly hostile, passive-aggressive, etc. (at least three examples):

_____

_____

_____

8. **Finances**—We handle our financial resources much like our emotional ones. Thus, when your checking account is unbalanced, or worse, overdrawn, or bills are overdue, or there is no cash in your pocket, or you are spending more than you earn, your financial overextension may parallel your emotional bankruptcy. List the signs that show when you are financially overextended (at least three examples):

_____

_____

_____

9. **Spiritual Life and Personal Reflection**—Spirituality can be diverse and include such methods as meditation, yoga, and prayer. Personal reflection includes keeping a personal journal, working the Twelve Step program with daily readings, and therapy. What are sources of routine personal reflection that are neglected when you are overextended? (at least three examples):

_____

_____

_____

10. **Other Addictions or Symptom Behaviors**—Compulsive behaviors which have negative consequences are symptomatic of your general well-being or the state of your overall recovery. When you watch inordinate amounts of TV, overeat, bite your nails—any habit you feel bad about afterward—these can be signs of burnout or possible relapse. Symptom behaviors are behaviors which are evidence of overextension, such as forgetfulness, slips of the tongue or jealousy. What negative addiction or symptom behaviors are present when you are "on the edge"? (at least three examples):

_____

_____

_____

PERSONAL CRAZINESS INDEX
Part Two–Recording Your PCI

The PCI is effective only when a careful record is maintained. Recording your daily progress in conjunction with regular journal keeping will help you to: keep focused on priorities which keep life manageable; work on program efforts a day at a time; expand your knowledge of personal patterns; provide a warning in periods of vulnerability to self-destructive cycles or addictive relapse.

From the thirty or more signs of personal craziness you recorded, choose the seven that are most critical for you. At the end of each day, review the list of seven key signs and count the ones you did that day, giving each behavior one point. Record your total for that day in the space provided on the chart. If you fail to record the number of points for each day, that day receives an automatic score of 7. (*If you cannot even do your score, you are obviously out of balance.*) At the end of the week, total your seven daily scores and make an X on the graph. Pause and reflect on where you are in your recovery. Chart your progress over a 12-week period.

My seven key signs of personal craziness:

1. _____

2. _____

3. _____

4. _____

5. _____

6. _____

7. _____

PCI Chart

© 1988 Patrick Carnes, Ph.D.

Day	Week	1	2	3	4	5	6	7	8	9	10	11	12
Sunday													
Monday													
Tuesday													
Wednesday													
Thursday													
Friday													
Saturday													
Weekly Total													

PCI Graph

50

48
46   Very High Risk
44
42

40

38
36   High Risk
34
32

30

28
26   Medium Risk
24
22

20

18
16   Stable Solidity
14
12

10

8
6   Optimum Health
4
2

0

Interpretation of the PCI

A guideline for understanding your score is suggested below:

Optimum Health
0-9

Knows limits; has clear priorities; congruent with values; rooted in diversity; supportive; has established a personal system; balanced, orderly, resolves crises quickly; capacity to sustain spontaneity; shows creative discipline.

Stable Solidity
10-19

Recognizes human limits; does not pretend to be more than he or she is; maintains most boundaries; well ordered; typically feels competent, feels supported, able to weather crisis.

Medium Risk
20-29

Slipping; often rushed; can't get it all in; no emotional margin for crisis; vulnerable to slip into old patterns; typically lives as if has inordinate influence over others and/or feels inadequate.

High Risk
30-39

Living in extremes (overactive or inactive); relationships abbreviated; feels irresponsible and is; constantly has reasons for not following through; lives one way, talks another; works hard to catch up.

Very High Risk
40-49

Usually pursuing self-destructive behavior; often totally into mission or cause or project; blames others for failures; seldom produces on time; controversial in community; success- vs. achievement-oriented.

Reflection on the Sixth and Seventh Steps

Beyond a wholesome discipline,
be gentle with yourself.
You are a child of the universe,
no less than the trees and the stars;
you have a right to be here.
And whether or not it is clear to you,
no doubt the universe
is unfolding as it should.

— Desiderata

Reflect on the words above and think of what gentleness you need for yourself at this point. While you turn over your imperfections, it helps to remember your goodness and acknowledge the higher order. Record your thoughts here.

Step Eight

Made a list
of all persons we had harmed,
and became willing
to make amends to all of them.

Step Nine

Made direct amends to such people
wherever possible,
except when to do so
would injure them or others.

Besides asking for help from your Higher Power for your shortcomings, you can act on your own to mend the harm you have caused as part of your illness. In Step Eight you identify people harmed, and in Step Nine you actually make the amends necessary. When finished with Step Nine, you will have done all you can and can turn over any remaining shame and guilt. The principles of forgiveness and restitution will become an ongoing part of living your life.

Reflecting on all levels of your awareness is very important to a thorough Eighth Step. When making your list of the persons you have harmed, consider the following:

— The name of the **person** who has been harmed. Don't concentrate only on those people who are closest to you. In casual relationships or acquaintances there was harm done as well.

— **Memories** of harm done. Record the specifics that you remember about the harm, including your behavior and the other person's reactions. Include facial expressions, tones of voice, circumstances, or anything that will make clear what happened.

— **Thoughts** about the harm. Ask yourself what you think about the situation now. Do you have reflections or interpretations about the harm?

— **Feelings** about the harm. Acknowledge the pain, anger, shame, guilt and fear that you have about the situation now. Also ask yourself what feelings you have about attempting to repair the damage.

— **Intentions** you now have. Perhaps the hardest part is to determine what you really hope to accomplish by doing some repair work. Sometimes our intentions are not helpful. If, for example, your intent is to look good to others, you probably need to take a longer look at your motives.

— **Amends** you can make for the harm caused. Name specific actions that will make up for what happened. Sometimes that may mean simply saying "I'm sorry." You will find some situations for which nothing can be done: for example, you have no idea how to reach someone, and the only amend you can make is to live your life differently. In some situations, further contact might cause further harm. At least you will be able to integrate that fact into your self-awareness. At the conclusion, you will have a list of all the amends you are willing to make. You will also have some blank spaces when it comes to amends.

As you can see, this will be a lengthy, difficult, soul-searching process that requires creativity and courage. Your guides can be important here. By reviewing your process as you go along, they can help you stay in reality. Maybe they will have different reactions to the events than you have, or perhaps they will challenge your intentions or suggest alternative actions. Remember, these amends do not have to be done all at once. You deserve time to think and to feel the process through. Again, gentleness is your goal.

The next several pages provide a worksheet for you to use. On the far right is a space labeled "date." As you make each amend, record the date it was completed. By updating the column you will know exactly where you are on your Ninth Step. Entering the dates will remind you to call your guides and update them as well.

RECORD OF THOSE HARMED AND AMENDS MADE

Person

Memories of Harm:

Thoughts:

Feelings:

Intentions:

Amends:

Date:

RECORD OF THOSE HARMED AND AMENDS MADE (cont'd.)

Person _____

Memories of Harm:
_____
_____
_____

Thoughts:
_____
_____

Feelings:
_____
_____

Intentions:
_____
_____

Amends:
_____
_____

Date: _____

RECORD OF THOSE HARMED AND AMENDS MADE (cont'd.)

Person _____

Memories of Harm:

Thoughts:

Feelings:

Intentions:

Amends:

Date:

RECORD OF THOSE HARMED AND AMENDS MADE (cont'd.)

Person _____

Memories of Harm: _____
_____

Thoughts: _____
_____

Feelings: _____
_____

Intentions: _____
_____

Amends: _____
_____

Date: _____

RECORD OF THOSE HARMED AND AMENDS MADE (cont'd.)

Person

Memories of Harm:

Thoughts:

Feelings:

Intentions:

Amends:

Date:

RECORD OF THOSE HARMED AND AMENDS MADE (cont'd.)

Person _____

Memories of Harm:

_____

_____

_____

Thoughts:

_____

_____

Feelings:

_____

_____

Intentions:

_____

_____

Amends:

_____

_____

Date: _____

If we are painstaking about this phase of our
development, we will be amazed before we are
halfway through. We are going to know a new
freedom and a new happiness.
We will not regret the past nor wish to shut the
door on it. We will comprehend the word
serenity and we will know peace.
No matter how far down the scale we have gone,
we will see how our experience can benefit others.
That feeling of uselessness and self-pity
will disappear. We will lose interest in selfish
things and gain interest in our fellows.
Self-seeking will slip away.
Our whole attitude and outlook upon life
will change. Fear of people and of economic
insecurity will leave us. We will intuitively know
how to handle situations which used to baffle us.
We will suddenly realize that God is doing for us
what we could not do for ourselves.

Alcoholics Anonymous — The "Big Book"

These are the famous promises of the program. Reflect on completing your
Eighth and Ninth Steps.

Guides: What examples of the promises at work do you see in the life of this workbook owner?

Record your reactions here:

Guide name: _____ Date:_____

Step Ten

Continued to take
personal inventory, and
when we were wrong,
promptly admitted it.

Step Eleven

Sought through prayer and meditation to improve
our conscious contact with God *as we understood Him,*
praying only for knowledge of His will for us
and the power to carry that through.

Steps Ten and Eleven ask you to integrate the program principles of honesty and spiritual exploration into your daily life. By now you will have noticed that the program asks you at different points to be a list maker. Making lists becomes one way for you to develop personal awareness. Daily monitoring of the realities of your strengths and limitations plus being willing to acknowledge your failings and successes is the surest path to sanity. From the beginning of this workbook we have emphasized balance, focus, and self-responsibility. Applying those concepts to Step Ten we see:

Balance—acknowledging strengths and limitations.

Focus—daily personal inventory.

Self-responsibility—acknowledging successes and failures promptly.

This commitment to integrity lays the foundation for active spirituality. Conversely, such rigorous ongoing self-examination can only be sustained with a strong spiritual base—Step Eleven. The combination of the two becomes a way of life for program people. The spiritual component grows through daily readings, meditation, prayer, and journal writing.

BALANCED EQUATIONS:
A Ten-Day Exercise for Steps Ten and Eleven

In the following exercise, ten equations are provided which represent the essential but delicate balance we all need in our lives. The first equation, the happiness equation, is taken from Dan Millman's *Way of the Peaceful Warrior;* it served as the inspiration for this exercise. These equations are illustrations of the relative components of these key recovery issues:

— Happiness

— Growth

— Serenity

— Peace of mind

— Reality

— Achievement

— Intimacy

— Productivity

— Health

— Spirituality

Use each equation as a daily meditation upon imbalances in your life. Record your reflections and then compose a prayer for each day—a prayer which helps you strike a balance.

At the end of the ten days, have a discussion with your guides about what process you would like to develop and use to maintain your conscious contact with God. Spirituality is a fundamentally personal and dynamic process. In addition to daily meditation and prayer, your plan to keep your connection to your Higher Power may include any practices—from helping others to sitting by a stream—that work for you.

■ HAPPINESS = $\dfrac{\text{Satisfaction}}{\text{Desires}}$

DAY ONE

Happiness exists when what you want is matched by what you have. If your desires are few, they are easy to satisfy.

Are you so obsessed with what you do not have that you miss what you have now? Are your desires so intense that you always have to be striving for more to satisfy them?

Reflection: _____

_____

_____

_____

_____

_____

_____

_____

_____

_____

_____

_____

_____

_____

_____

_____

_____

_____

_____

_____

_____

Prayer

GROWTH = $\dfrac{\text{Change}}{\text{Stability}}$

DAY TWO

Systems need to change or they die. Change is an essential ingredient to growth. Change without a stable foundation, however, leads to chaos. Any recovery program has elements of change as well as elements of stability.

Do you have a stable foundation to support your growth? Are you afraid to risk change, remaining stuck where you are?

Reflection: _____

_____

_____

_____

_____

_____

_____

_____

_____

_____

_____

_____

_____

_____

_____

_____

_____

_____

Prayer

SERENITY = $\dfrac{\text{Boundaries}}{\text{Options}}$

DAY THREE

Addicts and co-addicts live in the extremes, which means they can take any option to an excess. Imposing limits in the form of boundaries creates balance. The Serenity Prayer epitomizes this principle by praying for courage "to change the things I can."

Do you pursue all your possibilities without any limits? Are you too caring, too helpful, too involved, too committed, too generous, etc.?

Reflection: _____

_____

_____

_____

_____

_____

_____

_____

_____

_____

_____

_____

_____

_____

_____

_____

Prayer

▜ PEACE OF MIND = $\dfrac{\text{Known to Others}}{\text{Known to Self}}$

DAY FOUR

Anxiety originates in secrets about yourself that others do not know. Worry about others discovering the truth destroys your peace of mind. When there are others in your life who know all there is to know, you can be peaceful and stop living in terror of another abandonment.

Are you living in fear because of untold secrets? Have you lied to people because you wanted to avoid conflict or hurting someone? Have you friends you can confide your fear to?

Reflection: _____

_____

_____

_____

_____

_____

_____

_____

_____

_____

_____

_____

_____

_____

_____

_____

_____

Prayer

REALITY = $\dfrac{\text{Light Side}}{\text{Dark Side}}$

DAY FIVE

Reality is acknowledging both your strengths and your weaknesses. To focus on only your failures distorts reality. To see only the successes equally blurs your vision. Both need to be fully—not partially—acknowledged and accepted.

Do you have more difficulty admitting strengths or weaknesses? Do you fully admit that you have both?

Reflection: _____

_____

_____

_____

_____

_____

_____

_____

_____

_____

_____

_____

_____

_____

_____

_____

_____

_____

Prayer

_____

◢ ACHIEVEMENT = $\dfrac{\text{Vision}}{\text{Plan}}$

DAY SIX

Genuine achievement combines both an image of what needs to be done and a concrete plan of action to get the tasks done. A plan without vision goes nowhere. A vision without concrete action never becomes reality. Part of thinking "a day at a time" is to break a dream into little pieces that can be done a "piece" at a time.

Do you procrastinate about taking action on your ideas? Do you think about what you want to do before acting? Do you break big dreams into daily, doable pieces?

Reflection: _____

_____

_____

_____

_____

_____

_____

_____

_____

_____

_____

_____

_____

Prayer

_____
_____
_____
_____
_____
_____
_____
_____
_____
_____
_____
_____
_____
_____
_____
_____
_____
_____
_____
_____
_____
_____
_____
_____
_____
_____

INTIMACY = $\dfrac{\text{Fidelity to Others}}{\text{Fidelity to Self}}$

DAY SEVEN

Ultimately, intimacy exists because of trust. When fidelity to yourself matches faithfulness to others, trust occurs. People who report clearly their own needs, boundaries, and feelings are trustable. You can predict—or trust—what they will do. If you are accountable to others, people will feel safe being close to you.

Do you compromise yourself or give in too easily and then get mad? Do you say yes when you really want to say no? Do you follow through on your promises? Can people trust you enough to be intimate?

Reflection: _____

_____

_____

_____

_____

_____

_____

_____

_____

_____

_____

_____

_____

_____

_____

Prayer

PRODUCTIVITY = $\frac{Being}{Doing}$

DAY EIGHT

Truly productive people also take time to re-create themselves by doing nothing. Stopping to enjoy all that is around is essential to renewing your energy. What you do needs to be matched by times of simply being.

Do you stop to smell the flowers? Do you have "busy" vacations? Do you have daily downtime? Do you take time to be quiet? Are you meditating too much and not accomplishing anything concrete?

Reflection: _____

_____

_____

_____

_____

_____

_____

_____

_____

_____

_____

_____

_____

_____

_____

_____

_____

Prayer

HEALTH = $\dfrac{\text{Awareness}}{\text{Practice}}$

DAY NINE

As a recovering person, you need to take greater responsibility for your health. This means you need to learn about it and develop your awareness. Your awareness must be matched by action. Do you do what you know you should?

Are there aspects of your own health you need to know more about? Do you take care of yourself physically and respect your body? Are you doing what you need to?

Reflection: _____

_____

_____

_____

_____

_____

_____

_____

_____

_____

_____

_____

_____

_____

_____

_____

_____

Prayer

_____

■ SPIRITUALITY = $\dfrac{\text{Mortality}}{\text{Meaning}}$

DAY TEN

Spirituality starts with understanding your own human limitations, beginning with your mortality. Given those limits, you need to explore what meaning they have for you. Philosophical speculation without the reality of your human limits has no foundation and quickly becomes irrelevant. And daily life becomes pointless without a sense of higher purpose.

Do you live each day as if it were your last? How do you respond to pain and suffering in the world and in your life?

Reflection: _____

_____

_____

_____

_____

_____

_____

_____

_____

_____

_____

_____

_____

_____

_____

_____

_____

_____

_____

Prayer

We must always hold truth,
as best we can determine it,
to be more important, more vital
to our self-interest, than our comfort.
Conversely, we must always consider
our personal discomfort
relatively unimportant and, indeed,
even welcome it in the service
of the search for truth.
Mental health is an ongoing process
of dedication to reality at all costs...
What does a life of total dedication
to truth mean?
It means, first of all, a life of continuous
and never ending stringent
self-examination.

— M. Scott Peck, M.D.
The Road Less Traveled

Reflect on the words of Scott Peck and think of your daily meditation and prayer practices. Do they help you maintain conscious contact with your Higher Power? Do they help you with your ongoing personal inventory?

NOTES

Guides: What do you see happening on a daily basis in the life of this workbook owner? Share your insights, feelings, and suggestions here.

Guide name: _____ Date: _____

12

Step Twelve

Having had a spiritual awakening
as the result of these steps,
we tried to carry this message to others,
and to practice these principles in all our affairs.

Helping others is a significant part of the program, and there are many ways the program gets passed on. When you live the program and share it with others, you are carrying the message, especially when you sponsor new members. In practicing the Twelfth Step you will find that —

— By witnessing to others, your appreciation of the program and the program's impact on your life deepens.

— By hearing the stories of new members, you are reminded of where you were when you started.

— By modeling to others, you become aware that you need to practice what you preach.

— By giving to others, you develop bonds with new people who really need you.

— By helping others, you give what you have received.

— By supporting new beginnings, you revitalize your own efforts.

Being a sponsor sounds intimidating, but there are only a few things you need to do:

— Work hard to understand your sponsee's whole story.

— Support your sponsee emotionally during those difficult times.

— Teach your sponsee about the basics of your particular program.

— Help your sponsee to focus on the steps of the program.

— Be honest with your sponsee about how you see him or her working the program.

In your relationships with those you sponsor, you will be finding good things about them that they overlook. (Remember when all you could find to report to your sponsor was the latest disaster?) You will work hard to help new members see what it is they are doing right. Addicts and co-addicts, by definition, see only the bad in themselves. Perhaps the most priceless gifts a sponsor can give are those beginning affirmations.

As a sponsor you serve as a special role model. How you work your program will have a significant impact on those you help. To bolster your confidence, have your guides share their reactions to your being a sponsor using the space provided on page 200.

You also need to be very clear about your own definition of sobriety. To review that again will help you be more clear with your sponsee. No doubt your understanding of your sobriety has evolved since those early days when you told the group what you would *not* do. The sobriety worksheet provided reflects the old Buddhist axiom that wisdom is being able to say yes as well as no. In sobriety terms, this means that recovery is more than abstinence from self-destructive behavior. It is also a positive statement about what you embrace as well.

Much of this has probably been clear to you for some time, but to record and discuss your personal standards of sobriety with your own guides will be helpful for you and for those you are about to help.

Remember, your path is gentle. You can get help in learning to help others. Your Higher Power will be with you.

Now proceed to your guide affirmation sheet.

TWELFTH STEP GUIDE AFFIRMATIONS

The purpose of this page is for your guides to affirm you and your suitability to help others on the gentle path.

Note to guides and friends: As you list affirmations, the more specific you can be, the more helpful the affirmations will be.

Example: You are one of the best listeners I know. S. K.

1. _____

2. _____

3. _____

4. _____

5. _____

6. _____

7. _____

8. _____

9. _____

10. _____

11. _____

12. _____

13. _____

14. _____

15. _____

SOBRIETY WORKSHEET

Now that you have come this far along the gentle path, it's time to create a sobriety worksheet to keep your recovery on course. This worksheet will be an exceptionally valuable tool to use as a reference guide in the weeks and months to come. Review it regularly.

Here are the basic directions with some very simple examples:

1. Brainstorm and then list your **personal sobriety boundaries and danger zones,** being as specific as you can.

    Example: Boundaries: Drinking any alcohol. Smoking pot.
    Danger Zones: Getting too hungry, angry, lonely or tired.
    Talking to my parents about certain touchy subjects.

2. Choose those **boundaries that are most important to your sobriety** and record on the line labeled "Sobriety Boundary."

    Example: Drinking any alcohol.

3. On the diagrams beginning on page 203, for each individual boundary, record the actual **behaviors that would constitute a slip** and require a revision of your sobriety date. Focus on those specific behaviors that were part of your addictive life. Record on the line labeled "Ø."

    Example: Drinking beer at my favorite bar.

4. Next, list the **behaviors that** are not actual slips, but **would detract from or compromise your sobriety.** These are the behaviors that usually occurred before the actual addictive behavior. In other words, these are the things you usually did before a certain acting out or binge. Realizing this, you also know that these are potentially seductive behaviors and can lead you into a real danger zone. Record on the line labeled "—."

    Example: Going to my favorite bar, but not drinking beer.

5. For many addictions, or maybe for every one, fantasy is an integral part of the addictive experience. Whether excessive daydreaming, fantasizing, or actual trance-like preoccupation, these mental states are conducive to engaging in the old bad habits. Remembering that you alone know your obsessive thoughts and that only you are responsible for protecting your sobriety, list those **fantasies that are unhealthy for you.** Record on the line labeled "F."

    Example: Reminiscing about good times and good beer at my favorite bar.

6. Finally, record those **positive actions you now know will affirm or strengthen your sobriety boundaries.** These behaviors will serve as survival action steps to help you through the difficult times that are bound to come on the path to sobriety and serenity. Don't forget to state what you will work *for.* Record on the line labeled "⊕."

    Example: When I begin thinking about going to my favorite bar, I will call my sponsor. I will schedule regular activities with good friends that don't drink.

My Sobriety Date: _____

My Personal Sobriety Boundaries:

_____

_____

_____

_____

Danger Zones:

_____

_____

_____

_____

SOBRIETY WORKSHEET (cont'd)

1.

Sobriety Boundary

Ø
Behavior that Equals a Slip

—
Behavior that Compromises Sobriety

F
Fantasy

⊕

Action Step to Strengthen, Affirm Sobriety

2.

Sobriety Boundary

Ø
Behavior that Equals a Slip

—
Behavior that Compromises Sobriety

F
Fantasy

⊕

Action Step to Strengthen, Affirm Sobriety

SOBRIETY WORKSHEET (cont'd)

3.

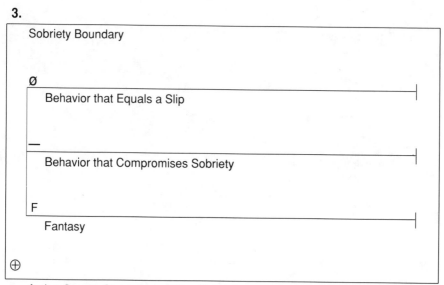

Sobriety Boundary

Ø

Behavior that Equals a Slip

—

Behavior that Compromises Sobriety

F

Fantasy

⊕

Action Step to Strengthen, Affirm Sobriety

4.

Sobriety Boundary

Ø

Behavior that Equals a Slip

—

Behavior that Compromises Sobriety

F

Fantasy

⊕

Action Step to Strengthen, Affirm Sobriety

Denial is the hallmark
of the immature, the insecure,
the self-centered, the non-affirmed.
When Faust, the man who was
willing to sell his soul
to the devil and condemn
himself to hell,
asked his visitor who he was,
Mephistopheles replied,
"I am the spirit
who always denies!"

— Conrad Baars, M.D.
Born Only Once

The Twelfth Step requires that you share your path with others. The joy of your sobriety and its life-giving reality are what you have to give. Denial is how you have lost your way in the past. Reflect on the quote above and think about how the Twelfth Step can maintain reality in your life. Think too about the contrast between the gift you offer new members and the offer of Mephistopheles.

Getting This Far

Getting this far means you have worked very hard and have given many gifts to yourself. You have by now integrated Twelve Step principles into your core being, have changed your life dramatically, and have a rich community of friends. Let the workbook be a record of your transformation and a celebration of your courage.

There may come a time when you feel the need to revitalize your program. You may wish to complete the workbook again. People report that using these exercises at different times in their lives generated very different experiences. Feel free to repeat them. All you need is the desire, the courage, and some blank sheets of paper.

By now you've probably realized that there is no finish line on the gentle path through the Twelve Steps. The steps are a process, ongoing, regenerating, renewing. In recovery, as in life generally, there are always new challenges, and you will find, if you keep reaching out, plenty of friends along the way.

My congratulations!

Patrick J. Carnes

Suggested Reading

Alcoholics Anonymous World Services, Inc., *Alcoholics Anonymous, Third Edition* (New York City, 1976).

Alcoholics Anonymous World Services, Inc., *Twelve Steps and Twelve Traditions* (New York City, 1978).

Anonymous, *Hope and Recovery, A Twelve Step guide for healing from compulsive sexual behavior* (Minneapolis: CompCare Publishers, 1987).

B., Bill, *Compulsive Overeater* (Minneapolis: CompCare Publishers, 1981).

Becker, Ernest, *The Denial of Death* (New York: The Free Press, 1973).

Carnes, Patrick, *Out of the Shadows: Understanding Sexual Addiction* (Minneapolis: CompCare Publishers, 1983).

Fossum, Merle A., and Mason, Marilyn J., *Facing Shame: Families in Recovery* (New York: W.W. Norton & Company, 1986).

Grateful Members of Emotional Health Anonymous, *The Twelve Steps for Everyone...who really wants them*, revised edition (Minneapolis: CompCare Publishers, 1987).

McGill, Michael E., Ph.D., *The McGill Report on Male Intimacy* (New York: Harper & Row Publishers, 1985).

Miller, Sherod, Nunally, Elam W., and Wackman, David B., *Couple Communication, Talking Together* (Littleton, CO: Interpersonal Communication Programs, 1979).

Millman, Dan, *Way of the Peaceful Warrior* (Tiburon, CA: H. J. Kramer, Inc., 1984).

Nouwen, Henri J.M., *Reaching Out* (New York: Doubleday & Company, 1975).

Paul, Jordan, Ph.D., and Paul, Margaret, Ph.D., *Do I Have To Give Up Me To Be Loved By You?* (Minneapolis: CompCare Publishers, 1983).

Peck, M. Scott, M.D., *The Road Less Traveled* (New York: Simon & Schuster, Inc., 1978).

Rubin, Lillian B., *Intimate Strangers* (New York: Harper & Row Publishers, 1983).

Sheperd, Scott, Ph.D., *Survival Handbook for the Newly Recovering* (Minneapolis: CompCare Publishers, 1988).

Twelve Step Support Group Information

The following is a partial list of Twelve Step groups.

Alcoholics Anonymous World Services, Inc.
Box 459, Grand Central Station
New York, NY 10017
(212) 686-1100

Al-Anon Family Groups
P.O. Box 862, Midtown Station
New York, NY 10118
(212) 302-7240

Co-Sex Addicts (Co-SA)
Twin Cities Co-S.A.
P.O. Box 14537
Minneapolis, MN 55414
(612) 537-6904

Debtors Anonymous National Organization
P.O. Box 20322
New York, NY 10025-9992

Emotional Health Anonymous
World Service Office
2420 San Gabriel Blvd.
Rosemead, CA 91770
(818) 573-5482
(213) 283-3574

Gamblers Anonymous
National Service Office
P.O. Box 17173
Los Angeles, CA 90017
(213) 386-8789

Narcotics Anonymous
> World Service Office
> P.O. Box 9999
> Van Nuys, CA 91409
> (818) 780-3951

Overeaters Anonymous
> 4025 Spencer, #203
> Torrance, CA 90503
> (213) 542-8363

Sexaholics Anonymous (SA)
> International Central Office
> P.O. Box 300
> Simi Valley, CA 93062
> (818) 704-9854
>
> P.O. Box 1542
> New York, NY 10185
> (212) 570-7292

Sex and Love Addicts Anonymous (SLAA)
> P.O. Box 1964
> Boston, MA 02105
> (617) 625-7961

Sexual Addicts Anonymous (SAA)
> Twin Cities Sexual Addicts Anonymous
> P.O. Box 3038
> Minneapolis, MN 55403
> (612) 339-0217

A Gentle Path through the Twelve Steps consists of a 212-page guidebook and an album containing six cassettes. You can order copies of the book and album separately or as a set at your bookstore or from the publisher.

To order by phone from CompCare Publishers: Call 1-800-328-3330. In Minnesota call 612-559-4800 collect. Charge orders only please.

Or order by mail using the form below.

Please send me:

☐ Workbook(s)   @ $9.95 ea. = $ _____
  (catalog no. 0373100-GP)

☐ Cassette Album(s)   @ $49.95 ea. = $ _____
  (catalog no. 8377400-GP)

☐ Workbook & Album sets   @ $55.00 ea. = $ _____
  (catalog no. 8378200-GP)

SUBTOTAL $ _____

Postage & Handling Charges

POSTAGE/HANDLING $ _____

Amount of Order	Charge
Up to $10.00	$ 2.00
$10.01 to $50.00	$ 3.50
$50.01 and over	$ 5.00

YOUR STATE SALES TAX $ _____

GRAND TOTAL $ _____

☐ Check enclosed, payable to CompCare Publishers.

☐ Charge my credit card:

_____ VISA _____ MC

ACCT NO. _____ EXP: _____

NAME _____

ADDRESS _____

ZIP _____

Mail to CompCare Publishers, 2415 Annapolis Lane, Minneapolis, MN 55441